The
CRAFT BEER
BITES
Cookbook

The CRAFT BEER BITES Cookbook

100 RECIPES FOR SLIDERS, SKEWERS, MINI DESSERTS, AND MORE—*All Made with Beer*

Jacquelyn Dodd

AUTHOR OF
The Craft Beer Cookbook

Adams Media
New York   London   Toronto   Sydney   New Delhi

Adams Media
An Imprint of Simon & Schuster, Inc.
57 Littlefield Street
Avon, Massachusetts 02322
Copyright © 2015 by Jacquelyn Dodd.

ADAMS MEDIA and colophon are trademarks of Simon and Schuster.

For information about special discounts for bulk purchases, please contact Simon & Schuster Special Sales at 1-866-506-1949 or business@simonandschuster.com.

The Simon & Schuster Speakers Bureau can bring authors to your live event. For more information or to book an event contact the Simon & Schuster Speakers Bureau at 1-866-248-3049 or visit our website at www.simonspeakers.com.

Photographs by Jacquelyn Dodd

Manufactured in the United States of America

10 9 8 7 6 5 4 3

Library of Congress Cataloging-in-Publication Data has been applied for.

ISBN 978-1-4405-8167-0
ISBN 978-1-4405-8168-7 (ebook)

To Cori and Claire,
for keeping me going in the
most difficult year of my life.
I hope to someday give each
of you a fraction of what
you've given me.

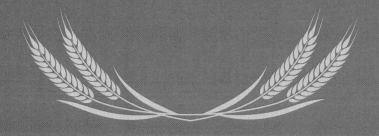

CONTENTS

Introduction . . . 11

Chapter 1: Cooking with Beer: Where to Begin . . . 13

Chapter 2: Getting Crafty: Craft Beer and Food . . . 17

Chapter 3

SLIDERS . . . 23

Barbecue Chicken Sliders with
Garlic Beer Pickles . . . 25

Beer-Battered Shrimp Po'Boy Sliders
with IPA Creole Mayo . . . 27

Beer-Braised Asian Pork Sliders with
Fried Wonton Buns . . . 29

Beer-Poached Lobster Sliders . . . 31

Crab Salad Sliders on Pepper Beer Biscuits . . . 32

Hawaiian IPA Pulled-Pork Sliders . . . 34

Mediterranean Beer-Braised Pork Sliders . . . 35

Pork Stout Meatball Banh Mi Sliders . . . 36

Porter Pulled-Pork Sliders with
Horseradish Guacamole . . . 37

Stout French Dip Sliders . . . 39

Chapter 4

SKEWERS . . . 41

Beer-Soaked Cantaloupe and
Mozzarella Skewers . . . 43

Grilled Beer-Marinated Prosciutto-Wrapped
Beef Tenderloin Skewers . . . 44

Grilled Rosemary Porter Fillet Tip Skewers . . . 45

Honey Stout Chicken Skewers . . . 47

IPA-Soaked Watermelon Skewers
with Cotija and Mint . . . 48

Maple Porter–Glazed Bacon-Wrapped Dates . . . 50

Roasted Garlic Beer Butter Shrimp Skewers . . . 52

Smoky Porter Molasses Chicken Skewers . . . 53

Stout-Marinated Beef Satay with
Beer Peanut Sauce . . . 57

Yogurt and Beer–Marinated
Chicken Skewers . . . 58

Chapter 5

CROSTINI . . . 59

Beer-Braised Carnitas Crostini . . . 61

Belgian Ale–Marinated Grilled Steak
Crostini with IPA Chimichurri . . . 63

Duck Confit Crostini with Porter Onion
Jam and Pomegranates . . . 65

Goat Cheese Crostini with Beer-
Pickled Peaches . . . 68

Porter Harissa Crostini . . . 69

Parmesan Crab Beer Cheese Crostini . . . 71

Peach Salsa and Beer-Battered
Avocado Crostini . . . 72

Smoked Salmon and Pale Ale Chive
Cream Cheese Crostini . . . 73

Spinach Artichoke Beer Cheese Crostini . . . 75

Stout-Soaked Mushroom and Herbed
Goat Cheese Crostini . . . 76

Chapter 6
DIPS . . . 77

Beer and Bacon Dip . . . 79

Buffalo Chicken Beer Cheese Dip . . . 80

Chipotle Porter Hummus . . . 81

Crispy Shallots and Parmesan
Beer Cheese Dip . . . 83

Pale Ale and Kale Tzatziki . . . 84

Parsley White Bean Beer Cheese Dip . . . 86

Porter Black Bean Dip . . . 87

Seven-Layer Jalapeño IPA Hummus Dip . . . 88

Triple-Chili Beer Cheese Dip . . . 89

Roasted Garlic and Smoked Porter
Baba Ghanoush . . . 90

Chapter 7
HAND PIES, WRAPS, & ROLLS . . . 93

Beer-Brined Chicken and Strawberry
Salsa Lettuce Wraps . . . 95

Beer Pesto and Beer Ricotta Mini Calzones . . . 96

Beer-Caramelized Mushroom and
Spinach Hand Pies . . . 98

Blackberry Stout Wontons . . . 99

Brown Ale Pork and Apple–Filled Buns . . . 100

Chicken Beer Cheese Pretzel Empanadas . . . 102

IPA Smoked Salmon Lettuce Wraps . . . 105

Mushroom Stout Pork Hand Pies . . . 106

Smoked Stout, Caramelized Onion,
and Potato Pierogies . . . 108

Tomato Beer Jam–Filled Biscuits . . . 109

Chapter 8
HANDFULS: NUTS, OLIVES, POPCORN . . . 111

Beer and Sriracha–Candied Nuts . . . 113

Beer-Battered Gorgonzola-Stuffed Olives . . . 115

Beer-Candied Pecans . . . 116

Beer Sausage–Stuffed Crispy Fried Olives . . . 117

Chili Lime Beer Roasted Peanuts . . . 118

Chocolate and Stout–Coated Almonds . . . 119

Curried Belgian Ale Mixed Nuts . . . 121

Cocoa and Stout Roasted Almonds . . . 122

Garlic Beer–Butter Popcorn . . . 123

Salted Beer Caramel Corn . . . 124

Chapter 9
TARTLETS AND MINI PIES . . . 125

Beer-Braised Lamb Shank Tarts with
Belgian Cherry Sauce . . . 127

Goat Cheese and Bacon Tarts with
Pale Ale Polenta Crust . . . 130

Belgian Ale–Caramelized Apple
and Onion Tarts . . . 131

Belgian Ale Ricotta Tarts with Roasted Figs
and Honey Beer Caramel Sauce . . . 134

Blackened Beer-Brined Chicken Masa
Tarts with IPA Guacamole . . . 138

Grilled Barbecue Chicken and
Peach Mini Pizzas . . . 140

Grilled Brie and Prosciutto Flatbreads with
Honey-Orange Beer Glaze . . . 142

Hoisin Stout–Braised Pork Rib Tarts . . . 145

Beer–Caramelized Mushroom
Gorgonzola Tart . . . **146**

Porter-Soaked Plum, Bacon, and
Arugula Tarts . . . **147**

Chapter 10
SEAFOOD BITES . . . 149

Drunk Shrimp Diablo . . . **151**

Beer and Butter-Poached Scallops with
Orange Lime Gremolata . . . **153**

Beer-Battered Crab Beignets . . . **155**

Beer-Steamed Clams with Linguiça . . . **156**

Garlic Chili Beer Butter Shrimp . . . **158**

Mango Shrimp IPA Ceviche in
Baked Wonton Cups . . . **159**

Grilled Prawns with Cilantro Lime
White Ale Vinaigrette . . . **161**

Miso Stout Salmon Spring Rolls . . . **162**

Salmon Meatballs with Asian Porter Sauce . . . **164**

Miso Ale–Glazed Shrimp . . . **166**

Chapter 11
DEEP-FRIED . . . 167

Beer-Battered Avocado Fries . . . **169**

Beer-Battered Mini Corn Dogs . . . **170**

Beer-Battered Shrimp with Chipotle
Lime Dipping Sauce . . . **171**

Beer-Battered Stout Pork Meatballs . . . **172**

Beer Churros with Chocolate Stout Sauce . . . **173**

Fried IPA Cheddar Mashed Potato Balls . . . **175**

Jalapeño Cheddar Beer Hush Puppies . . . **176**

Jalapeño Popper Beer Cheese Wontons . . . **177**

Raspberry Porter Jelly–Filled Beer Donuts . . . **178**

Tempura Beer-Battered Asparagus . . . **181**

Chapter 12
DESSERTS . . . 183

Belgian Ale Blackberry Sour
Cream Ice Cream . . . **185**

Barrel-Aged Stout Marshmallows with
Stout Chocolate Dipping Sauce . . . **186**

Blueberry Beer Mini Pies . . . **188**

Chocolate Stout Cupcakes with Chocolate
Stout Cream Cheese Frosting . . . **190**

Chocolate Stout Whoopie Pies with
Chocolate Cream Cheese Filling . . . **192**

Grilled Apricots with Saison Mascarpone
and Stout Balsamic Glaze . . . **195**

Peanut Butter Stout Mousse–
Topped Brownies . . . **196**

Miniature Coffee Stout Cinnamon Rolls . . . **198**

Miniature Hefeweizen Pound Cakes
with Beer Whipped Cream . . . **200**

IPA Lemon Bars . . . **202**

U.S./Metric Conversion Chart . . . 203
Appendix: Glossary of Beer Terms . . . 205
Index . . . 213

INTRODUCTION

The Craft Beer Bites Cookbook is about community. It's about the community we build over a good pint and good plate of food. It's about the people we welcome into our lives and into our homes, the ones who always make it to our parties, the ones who drive us to the airport in the early morning hours, the ones who show up to help us move, the people who cheer our successes and pat our backs even in failure. It's about how this community has been built and grown in the world of craft beer, in every tap house, brewery, homebrew club, and hop farm. The world of craft beer is as much as about the people who have built it as it is about the beer they make; that's what joins us all together in the love of a shared fascination.

The Craft Beer Bites Cookbook is about sharing food at parties and gatherings that celebrate the brew and bring people together. Use this book to explore craft beer, whether you're new to the scene or a seasoned pro. Use the recipes as an excuse to try a beer you've never had or as a way to showcase the flavors of a beer you're in love with. Use it as a way to throw a party, celebrate beer, and grow a community of your own. Long live beer, and beer people.

Chapter 1

COOKING WITH BEER: WHERE TO BEGIN

Why would you cook with beer? Why not just drink it like a normal person? There are several practical reasons to cook with beer that trump even the frivolous ability to set a plate of food down in the center of the table and proudly proclaim, "I put beer in this!" although that's reason enough to pop a pint and pour it into your stockpot.

Taste

The flavor of beer is why we are all here in the first place, isn't it? We've fallen in love with the taste of this fermented beverage and we can't get enough. The flavor of beer can translate into food in different ways—sometimes a mild hint, other times a large, bold presence on the palate. If you made a dish and the flavor was just too much beer for your tender taste buds, there are a few things you can do.

🍺 Just add less beer. But you didn't need me to tell you that. I have faith in your deductive reasoning skills; you could have figured that out on your own. Make sure if you use this completely obvious tactic that you balance the dish. Replace the beer you removed with a liquid that fits the food: milk, water, broth, unicorn tears.

🍺 Use a beer that's less hoppy. Beers with a strong hop presence show up in a dish with a vengeance, especially when reduced. Using a lower-hop beer (for instance replacing a high-hop beer like an IPA with a low-hop beer like a white ale) may give you the taste profile you were looking for.

🍺 If the problem you are having isn't necessarily the beer flavor, per se, but the bitterness it brings to the dish, you can try adding some sugar. Even in savory dishes a bit of sugar or molasses or honey can tame that bitterness and give you the right balance. What if the beer flavor isn't strong enough? If you haven't already guessed, it's the same advice I've already given, just in reverse.

🍺 Add more beer, obviously. Remove some of the other liquid you've used in the dish and replace it with beer—but you already knew that.

🍺 You can also use a hoppier beer, like an IPA, which will give you a stronger beer flavor in the final dish.

🍺 Reduce a beer to create a concentrated beer flavor. Cook 12 ounces of beer on the stove down to 1–2 tablespoons for a more concentrated beer flavor.

If you are unsure where to start when creating a beer recipe, err on the side of caution and add the beer with a light hand. Even if the flavor isn't where you want it, at least dinner will be edible.

Leavening

Leavening is a fancy word for making dough rise. Beer, although mild by itself in its bread-puffing powers, will increase the rise of bread dough, cakes, and other baked goods. It can't be used on its own as a substitute for active yeast, baking soda, or baking powder, but it will give you a lighter, puffier, more tender texture than any other liquid employed in baking when you use it in tandem with a strong leavening agent.

Have a favorite bread recipe that uses water? Just substitute beer for the water (my favorite is a bottle-conditioned wheat beer), and fall even more in love with that recipe. Making a chocolate cake? Use a stout to give it a fantastic rich flavor and moist but tender texture. Keep in mind that beer is fat-free, so if you are replacing a fatty liquid, like cream or whole milk, you need to compensate for that fat. Add about 1 tablespoon of vegetable oil for every ½ cup of beer you use as a replacement for a fattier liquid. Beer is such a fantastic baking liquid, you may never bake a sober loaf again.

Meat Tenderizing

Beer and meat have a long and glorious history together. Although there is no evidence to support me, I'd be willing to wager a six-pack that the first beer used in cooking was used to tenderize a tough cut of meat. Alcohol is a natural meat tenderizer, and beer has the right liquid-to-alcohol ratio to get the job done right without oversaturating the meat with the taste of alcohol. Different cuts of meat and cooking methods lend themselves better to various styles of beer. For brining a chicken or a turkey, look for a brown ale with notes of nuts or cloves. For braising beef or pork, grab a chipotle porter. For marinating a steak for the grill, go for a coffee stout. Fish works well with a citrusy white ale.

Odds and Ends

Alcohol intensifies heat, which can be good or bad. If you make a dish that's more mild than you had intended, pair it with a high-ABV (alcohol by volume) IPA to give that dish the right kick of heat that you want. When marinating a pepper in beer (for instance, if you're making ceviche or salsa), keep in mind that the alcohol in the beer will, for better or worse, exaggerate the impact of the capsaicin.

Due to the hops, beer is a mild preservative. This won't make your beer-cooked items last forever, but it will give that beer bread or porter onion jam a few more days in the fridge than you would have gotten without it. Hops were originally added to beer purely for the preservative powers they bring. It wasn't until later that those bitterly delicious little flowers were added more for taste than preservation.

Chapter 2

GETTING CRAFTY: CRAFT BEER AND FOOD

Craft beer has seen an epic rise in popularity in the past five years. This is reflected not just in the amount of beer being produced or the number of breweries opening every month in the United States but with the way quality craft beer has infiltrated mainstream culture. Whether it's celebrities showing up in gossip mags holding cans of their favorite local brew or craft beer glassware on display at several major upscale housewares chains, craft beer can't be ignored—it's a household word.

With this rise in awareness has come the tendency to celebrate beer in its best forms.

IPA Day is celebrated on the first Thursday in August with craft beer devotees breaking out their favorite high-hop beers and proudly sharing the fermented consumption via social media and hop-head gatherings at local pubs.

International Stout Day is celebrated in November when beer aficionados pour themselves a heady glass of dark deliciousness.

National Beer Day is celebrated on April 7, the day the law that Franklin D. Roosevelt signed as an amendment to the Volstead Act went into effect, which would eventually reverse Prohibition. With all of these beer-related holidays, the desire to celebrate with beer-themed parties is also on the rise. Beer parings are common, as are growler potlucks (growlers are large, legal, "to-go" containers that can be filled at local breweries) and cooking-with-beer parties. If you want to join in on the fun, where do you start? How do you throw a craft beer party?

Let's start with the basics.

How to Pair Beer and Food

Before we jump in to my treasure trove of beer-and-food-pairing tips, we need to dispel one myth: There are no rules. Drink what you prefer and eat likewise. If *you* like it, it's a good pairing; there are no hard and fast rules, just considerations and principles to keep in mind.

1. Consider intensity. When subjecting your tasters to a palate-wreaking chipotle dish or 1,000 IBU (International Bittering Units) IPA, consider what you're pairing that monster with. Mild works well with mild, and strong holds up next to strong. If you really want to pair an intense food or beer, you may consider an equally intense counterpart that can take a punch.

2. What flavors linger should be what's paired. When you think about what you can pair a food or a beer with, consider what flavors stick around on your palate after the bite. Making a steak with a garlicky cream sauce? That sauce will probably linger more than the meat. Pair to the sauce rather than the steak.

3. Alcohol intensifies heat. This can be good or bad, but it's a factor you should consider. Was that curry a little more mellow than you intended? Grab a high-ABV beer to kick the heat up a notch. On the other hand, that jalapeño and habanero chili might need a low-alcohol session beer.

4. Don't forget texture. I will spare you a lecture using my least-favorite beer term, "mouthfeel," and just mention that carbonation cuts through grease and fat. A great complement to a triple-cheese pizza isn't as much a flavor as a texture. Bubbles add a cleansing balance to a rich, greasy meal. On the other hand, a smooth stout, with low carbonation levels, will match the silkiness of a creamy chocolate mousse. Consider carbonation levels, not just flavors, when paring.

5. Think of all the flavors being in one bowl. The ingredients should be able to coexist simultaneously. Although an argument can be made for contrasting, it's good to start by complementing. The best way to do this is thinking about all the flavors together. Let's just pretend that you made yourself a big pot of homemade chicken noodle soup. What do you want to throw in that pot? A beer with notes of caramel and molasses or a beer with lemon and basil? I don't know about you, but that last beer is looking like a much better pairing for the job.

6. Do you pair with the beer you used in the dish? This one can be tricky. While it's never a bad pairing, it can encourage the flavors to get lost in your mouth. If you use a pumpkin beer in a pumpkin pie and pair it with that same pumpkin beer, you'll never be able to tease out which is which; it'll all just bleed together. It's like having a pink room with pink walls and pink carpet and pink bedding—it's just too damn much. Try a beer that complements rather than matches. For instance, if you want to serve a pumpkin ale, serve it with a pecan pie rather than a pumpkin pie. If you want to serve a pumpkin pie, pair it with a nut brown ale. Think about two flavors that go together rather than two flavors that match.

Craft Beer Party Themes

When it comes to throwing a craft beer party, you have an abundance of options. Craft beer is versatile and exciting with a broad spectrum of flavors that are just waiting to be explored and celebrated.

THE SEASONAL PARTY

Special-release beers are a year-round celebration of seasonal ingredients and the weather that goes along with them. Throw a party that highlights pumpkin beers, for instance, or maybe a celebration of summer saisons. Do a side-by-side taste test of different beers in the same style to see what you prefer and what you like to pair it with. Seasonal-release beers are generally brewed to pair well with the foods of that season. Raid your local farmers' market and make dishes that use in-season produce to pair with those special-release brews.

THE GROWLER POTLUCK

Invite your beer-loving friends over with one stipulation: They must bring a growler from a local taproom or brewery to share. You can let everyone bring what they like, or you can assign styles to make sure the spectrum is covered and there aren't too many of one style and not enough of another.

THE SUGAR SHINDIG

Do Chocolate Stout Cupcakes (see recipe in Chapter 12) go better with a chocolate stout, or is it a Belgian quad ale? Do you like a saison with IPA Lemon Bars (see recipe in Chapter 12), or do you want a pale ale? Make the desserts, try them with different beers, and decide what you like best. It's dessert and beer . . . there are no losers in this game.

SOME LIKE IT HOT

Play around with the alcohol-intensifying powers of beer with a spice-themed party. Make a slew of pepper-infused foods, and have your guest taste those dishes with three different beers: a pepper-infused beer (like a habanero pale ale or chipotle porter), a high-ABV IPA, and a very low-alcohol (session beer) pale ale. The different beers, especially the different alcohol levels, will drastically impact how spicy that food tastes.

All right. Now you're ready to wade into the world of beer bites. Good eating!

Chapter 3

SLIDERS

Barbecue Chicken Sliders with Garlic Beer Pickles . . . 25

Beer-Battered Shrimp Po'Boy Sliders with IPA Creole Mayo . . . 27

Beer-Braised Asian Pork Sliders with Fried Wonton Buns . . . 29

Beer-Poached Lobster Sliders . . . 31

Crab Salad Sliders on Pepper Beer Biscuits . . . 32

Hawaiian IPA Pulled-Pork Sliders . . . 34

Mediterranean Beer-Braised Pork Sliders . . . 35

Pork Stout Meatball Banh Mi Sliders . . . 36

Porter Pulled-Pork Sliders with Horseradish Guacamole . . . 37

Stout French Dip Sliders . . . 39

Barbecue CHICKEN SLIDERS WITH GARLIC BEER PICKLES

MAKES 24 SLIDERS

FOR THE PICKLES
1 pound Kirby cucumbers, sliced
10 cloves garlic, peeled
1 cup pale ale
1½ cups vinegar
¼ cups white sugar
2 tablespoons kosher salt
1 tablespoon black peppercorns
1 tablespoon whole allspice berries

FOR THE CHICKEN
1 tablespoon olive oil
4 cloves garlic, grated with a Microplane
⅓ cup low-sodium soy sauce
¼ cup tomato paste
1 tablespoon white vinegar
2 tablespoons Worcestershire sauce
2 teaspoons red chili sauce (such as sriracha)
2 teaspoons smoked paprika
12 ounces stout
⅓ cup brown sugar
2 teaspoons onion powder
2 pounds boneless, skinless chicken thighs
24 slider buns

Homemade pickles sound like a feat of culinary genius. They sound like something that requires skill and special tools, but in reality, it's a quick and simple process. But you can keep that last bit to yourself. Top your homemade chicken sliders with homemade pickles and let everyone wonder how you do it all.

1. In a small bowl, add the cucumbers and peeled garlic cloves; set aside.

2. In a saucepan over medium heat, add the beer, vinegar, sugar, salt, peppercorns, and allspice. Bring to a simmer just until the salt and sugar have dissolved, remove from the heat, and allow to cool to room temperature. Pour over the cucumbers and the garlic. Cover and refrigerate for at least 1 hour and up to 3 days.

3. Heat the olive oil in a saucepan over medium-high heat. Add the garlic and stir for 30 seconds; add the soy sauce, tomato paste, vinegar, Worcestershire sauce, red chili sauce, smoked paprika, stout, brown sugar, and onion powder. Simmer, stirring occasionally until thickened, about 8 minutes. Set aside.

4. Cook the chicken in a pot of lightly salted boiling water until cooked through, 10–15 minutes. Remove from the water and shred using two forks. Add the chicken to the barbecue sauce and toss to coat.

5. Fill the slider buns with barbecue chicken and a few slices of pickles.

(continued)

Beer-Battered SHRIMP PO'BOY
SLIDERS WITH IPA CREOLE MAYO

MAKES 12 SLIDERS

FOR THE SHRIMP
½ cup milk
½ cup IPA
1 pound raw shrimp, deveined, shell and
    tail removed
½ cup fine cornmeal
½ cup all-purpose flour
3 teaspoons creole seasoning
Pinch cayenne
Oil for frying

FOR THE MAYO
1 cup mayo
2 tablespoons IPA
1 teaspoon creole seasoning

FOR THE SLIDERS
12 French rolls, sliced to resemble slider
    buns
2 large tomatoes, sliced

The summer after I graduated high school I spent a few months as a lifeguard protecting adolescent campers from the depths of a murky lake. Three weeks in a busload of campers from New Orleans arrived, feisty and tan and ready to swim. Although they had a difficult time with the rules, they always made amends, mostly in the form of a green container of creole seasoning. All the kids had packed some alongside their swim attire when readying themselves for a week away from home. When I asked why, one brave kid offered the explanation, "Couldn't trust you West Coasters and all that ranch dressing you seem to put on everything. Needed to know I could make the food edible if I had to."

1. In a small bowl, stir together the milk and beer. Add the shrimp and allow to sit for 10 minutes.
2. In a separate bowl, stir together the cornmeal, flour, creole seasoning, and cayenne.
3. In a large skillet, add 2 inches of oil. Heat to 350°F using a cooking thermometer to maintain temperature.
4. A few at a time, remove the shrimp from the milk mixture, add to the flour mixture, and toss until well coated.
5. Add coated shrimp to the oil and fry on each side until golden brown, about 2 minutes per side. Remove and allow to drain on paper towels.
6. In a small bowl, stir together the mayo, IPA beer, and creole seasoning.
7. Spread the slider buns liberally with mayonnaise. Add 2 or 3 shrimp and a tomato slice to each bun.

(continued)

Choose the Right Brew!

This recipe needs the punch of a good IPA. Look for a hoppy beer with the brightness of fresh hops to give you the right balance.

Beer-Braised ASIAN PORK SLIDERS WITH FRIED WONTON BUNS

MAKES 12 MINI SLIDERS

12 ounces ground pork
1 clove garlic, minced
1 teaspoon fresh-grated ginger
2 tablespoons chopped scallions
½ teaspoon salt
2 tablespoons stout
2 tablespoons vegetable oil, plus more for frying
12 ounces wheat beer
24 wonton wrappers
¼ cup shredded carrots
¼ cup chopped cilantro
1 serrano chili, thinly sliced
¼ teaspoon sesame oil

Choose the Right Brew!

A nice big stout will lend a good punch to these little pork patties. Look for something with a little spice note to balance out the sweetness of the pork.

Not all sliders need a tiny burger bun. A fried wonton adds a nice crispy texture and an unexpected vehicle for a tasty little mini burger.

1. In a small bowl, add the pork, garlic, ginger, scallions, salt, and stout beer. Gently fold together until well combined.

2. Form into 12 small patties about 2½" wide and 1" high.

3. Heat 2 tablespoons oil in a pan over medium-high heat until hot but not smoking. Add the patties, cook on one side until brown, flip over, add the wheat beer, reduce heat to medium low, cover, and allow the patties to simmer until cooked through, about 8 minutes.

4. Remove from the pan and allow to drain on paper towels.

5. Using a 2" biscuit cutter, cut 24 circles out of the center of the wonton wrappers.

6. Heat about 2" of oil in a pan over high heat. Use a deep-fry thermometer to bring the oil to 350°F, adjusting the heat to maintain that temperature. A few at a time, fry the wonton circles until golden brown on each side, about 2 minutes. Remove from the oil; drain on a stack of paper towels.

7. In a small bowl, stir together the shredded carrots, cilantro, serrano chili, and sesame oil.

8. Plate the patties on a fried wonton circle, top with a pinch of the carrot mixture, and top with another wonton circle.

BEER-POACHED *Lobster Sliders*

3 lobster tails
1 lemon, cut into quarters
24 ounces pale ale
½ cup sour cream
Pinch cayenne
½ teaspoon black pepper
¼ cup chopped green onions
12 Hawaiian dinner rolls

Lobster tails are much more approachable than the whole beast. Although some like to look their dinner in the eye and show it who's the boss, most of us would rather have someone else do the dirty work. Buying tails that have been removed from the lobster by someone else seems to suit most of us much better. Especially when you decide those preremoved tails need a nice bath in some hot beer.

1. Using a sharp knife or kitchen shears, cut the lobster shells down the center lengthwise.

2. In a small saucepan, add the lobsters, lemon quarters, and enough beer until they are just submerged, making sure you have the right amount of liquid for poaching. Remove the lobster and bring the beer to a low simmer.

3. Add the lobster tails back into the pot and simmer until cooked through, about 6 minutes. Remove from the beer and allow to cool.

4. In a small bowl, stir together the sour cream, cayenne, black pepper, and green onions.

5. Remove the lobster meat from the shells, chop the meat, and gently fold into the sour cream mixture.

6. Fill the slider buns with the lobster mixture. Chill until ready to serve.

Choose the Right Brew!

An approachable pale ale with a nice malt-to-hops balance
will give you a tender lobster with just a hint of beer.

Crab Salad Sliders
ON PEPPER BEER BISCUITS

MAKES 8 SLIDERS

FOR THE BISCUITS
3½ cups all-purpose flour
2 teaspoons baking powder
1½ teaspoons baking soda
1 teaspoon salt
1 teaspoon sugar
1 teaspoon black pepper
8 tablespoons unsalted cold butter, cut into cubes
½ cup buttermilk
⅔ cup hefeweizen
2 tablespoons melted unsalted butter
1 teaspoon coarse sea salt

FOR THE CRAB SALAD
8 ounces crab leg meat
½ teaspoon Old Bay Seasoning
¼ teaspoon salt
½ teaspoon black pepper
¼ cup sour cream
2 teaspoons lemon zest
2 tablespoons chopped fresh flat-leaf parsley
¼ cup chopped tomatoes
2 tablespoons IPA

You can pretty much make any sandwich better with the addition of a homemade biscuit. A light, peppery biscuit is a great balance to the sweetness of the crab salad.

1. Preheat oven to 400°F.
2. In a food processor, add the flour, baking powder, baking soda, salt, sugar, and pepper. Pulse to combine. Add the cold butter; process until well combined. Add to a large bowl.
3. Add the buttermilk and beer. Mix with a fork until just combined. Add to a well-floured flat surface; pat into a rectangle. Using a cold rolling pin (preferably marble), gently roll into a large rectangle, about 1" in thickness, using as few strokes as possible.
4. Fold the dough into thirds as you would a letter about to go into an envelope. Roll lightly once in each direction to about 1" thickness; fold in thirds again. Gently roll to about 1½" thickness (this will give you the flaky layers).
5. Using a 2" biscuit cutter, cut out 8 biscuits. Place in a baking dish that has been sprayed with cooking spray.
6. Brush biscuits with melted butter; sprinkle sea salt. Bake for 12–15 minutes or until the tops are golden brown. Allow to cool completely.
7. In a large bowl, gently combine all the Crab Salad ingredients.
8. Split the biscuits and fill with Crab Salad.

(continued)

Choose the Right Brew!

For the biscuits, a nice wheat beer will give you a great texture. For the crab, grab a punchy IPA for a nice hop finish to the crab salad.

Hawaiian IPA PULLED-PORK SLIDERS

MAKES 24 SLIDERS

4 cloves garlic, roughly chopped
¼ cup low-sodium soy sauce
2 tablespoons Worcestershire sauce
¼ cup tomato paste
2 teaspoons sriracha
2 tablespoons brown sugar
2 cups chopped pineapple
3½ pounds pork shoulder
Salt and pepper
12 ounces IPA
24 Hawaiian rolls, split

I spent some time in Costa Rica a few years back. It didn't take long for my obsession with pineapple to reach a fevered pitch. The abundance of this tropical fruit made it practically free, and I'd order a "Piña y Agua" smoothie, paying fifty cents for 20 ounces of cold, liquefied pineapple several times a day. Back in the states, it just wasn't the same, but I couldn't stop thinking about ways to use one of my favorite fruits.

1. In a food processor or blender, add the garlic, soy sauce, Worcestershire sauce, tomato paste, sriracha, brown sugar, and pineapple. Process until well combined.

2. Place the pork shoulder inside a slow cooker; salt and pepper all sides liberally.

3. Pour the pineapple mixture and the IPA beer over the pork.

4. Cook on low for 8 hours.

5. Using two forks, shred while still in the slow cooker, discarding any large pieces of fat.

6. Allow to marinate in the juices for about 10 minutes; drain well. Serve inside split Hawaiian rolls.

Choose the Right Brew!

An IPA with a high ABV (alcohol by volume) will give you the right mix of beer flavor and meat-tenderizing abilities.

Mediterranean BEER-BRAISED PORK SLIDERS

MAKES 18 SLIDERS

The tang of a yogurt dressing does well to cut the richness of braised pork, and it adds a messy, get–your–hands–dirty element to these little treats.

FOR THE MEAT
1 tablespoon brown sugar
1 teaspoon smoked paprika
2 teaspoons salt
1 teaspoon onion powder
1 teaspoon garlic powder
1 teaspoon black pepper
1 teaspoon cumin
3 pounds country-style pork ribs
2 tablespoons olive oil
14½ ounces stewed tomatoes
12 ounces smoked porter
1 tablespoon Worcestershire sauce
1 white onion, chopped
3 cloves garlic, chopped

FOR THE TOPPING
1 cup plain Greek yogurt
2 tablespoons fresh lemon juice
2 tablespoons chopped dill
½ cup very thinly sliced red onion
18 slider buns
1 English cucumber, diced
1 cup chopped firm tomatoes

1. In a small bowl, stir together the brown sugar, smoked paprika, salt, onion powder, garlic powder, black pepper, and cumin.

2. Sprinkle pork on all sides with spice mixture.

3. Heat the olive oil over medium-high heat in a large Dutch oven until hot but not smoking. Sear pork on all sides, working in batches if necessary.

4. Pour the stewed tomatoes and beer over the pork. Add the Worcestershire, onions, and garlic. Reduce heat to a low simmer. Add a lid at a vent and allow to cook until pork is very tender and falling off the bone, about 4 hours. Shred using two forks, removing the bones from the pot. Remove meat from the pot with a slotted spoon to drain off excess moisture.

5. To make the sauce, whisk together the yogurt, lemon juice, dill, and red onion. Chill until ready to serve.

6. Split the burger buns and fill with pork; top with cucumber, tomatoes, and yogurt sauce.

Choose the Right Brew!

A rich, deep smoked porter will give a great
meaty flavor to this slow-cooked pork

Pork Stout MEATBALL
BANH MI SLIDERS

MAKES 12 SLIDERS

2 pounds ground pork
¼ cup stout
2 teaspoons fish sauce
½ teaspoon salt
1 teaspoon pepper
1 clove garlic, minced
2 teaspoons chopped fresh basil
2 tablespoons olive oil
2 tablespoons white vinegar
1 teaspoon sugar
1 tablespoon sesame oil
1 cup grated carrots
1 cup julienned daikon
¼ cup chopped cilantro
1 cup sour cream
2 teaspoons sriracha
12 crusty French dinner rolls, split

The first time I had a banh mi sandwich was at a taco truck in Los Angeles outside a beer event. Maybe it was the mélange of beer rolling around in my system, but it was the best damn sandwich I'd ever had. Since then, I'll order one if I see it on a menu. Add in the beer, which is how it will always be linked in my brain, and it's absolutely unforgettable.

1. In a medium bowl, stir together the pork, stout, fish sauce, salt, pepper, garlic, and basil. Form into balls slightly smaller than golf balls.
2. Heat the olive oil in a pan over medium-high heat. Add the meatballs and sauté until browned on all sides and cooked through, about 8 minutes.
3. In a small saucepan over medium-low heat, warm the vinegar; add the sugar and stir until dissolved. Add the sesame oil and allow to sit at room temperature until cooled.
4. In a small bowl, add the carrots, daikon, and cilantro. Drizzle the vinegar mixture over and toss to coat.
5. In a separate bowl, stir together the sour cream and sriracha.
6. Spread the inside of the buns with the sriracha sour cream. Add 2 meatballs to each roll and top with slaw.

Choose the Right Brew!

Dark beers, the stouts and porters, lend a deep richness to a pork dish. Look for one with notes of coffee, smoke, or spice.

Porter Pulled-Pork SLIDERS
WITH HORSERADISH GUACAMOLE

MAKES 24 SLIDERS

FOR THE PULLED PORK
1½ tablespoons kosher salt
1 tablespoon sugar
1 tablespoon onion powder
1 tablespoon chili powder
1 tablespoon ground cumin
1 tablespoon black pepper
2 teaspoons smoked paprika
2 teaspoons garlic powder
2 teaspoons dry mustard powder
3 pounds pork shoulder
3 tablespoons olive oil
22 ounces chipotle porter
2 cups beef stock

FOR THE HORSERADISH GUACAMOLE
2 large ripe Haas avocados
2 tablespoons fresh-squeezed lemon juice
½ teaspoon sea salt
1 teaspoon garlic powder
1 teaspoon onion powder
½ teaspoon cumin
1–2 tablespoons cream-style horseradish
24 slider buns

Pulled pork might be a staple in your house, and if it is, I hope it includes beer. But is horseradish guacamole a staple? It should be. You'll be hooked once you try it, especially with a rich meat like pulled pork.

1. In a small bowl, stir together the salt, sugar, onion powder, chili powder, cumin, pepper, smoked paprika, garlic powder, and mustard powder.

2. Sprinkle the pork on all sides with the spice mixture, pressing the spices into the meat.

3. In a large Dutch oven, heat the olive oil over medium-high heat until hot but not smoking. Add the pork shoulder; sear on all sides until browned. Pour the porter and stock over the pork; reduce heat to a simmer. Cover and allow to cook until tender and falling apart, 3–4 hours.

4. Using two forks, shred the pork. Allow the pork to sit in the braising liquid for 10 minutes, then drain (reserve the braising liquid for an alternate use, like making chili).

5. In a small bowl, add the avocados, lemon juice, salt, garlic powder, onion powder, cumin, and 1 tablespoon horseradish. Smash and stir with a fork until well combined. Add additional horseradish to taste.

6. Fill the slider buns with pulled pork and top with guacamole.

Choose the Right Brew!

A porter made with the nice, mellow heat of chipotle peppers
is perfect for these bold pulled-pork sliders.

Stout FRENCH DIP SLIDERS

MAKES 12 SLIDERS

1 tablespoon brown sugar
1 teaspoon black pepper
1 teaspoon salt
¼ teaspoon cayenne
¼ teaspoon smoked paprika
3 pounds chuck roast
2 tablespoons olive oil
12 ounces porter or stout
3 cups beef stock
12 French dinner rolls, split

If you live in Los Angeles, you know that there is a bit of a dispute over the invention of the French dip. You'll also know that it wasn't invented anywhere near France but in East L.A. Two restaurants, Cole's and Philippe the Original, lay claim to the humble beginnings of this classic sandwich, but neither includes beer, which, at this point, should be standard. They can fight over their sober sandwich; I'll take the beer version.

1. Preheat oven to 325°F.

2. In a small bowl, combine the brown sugar, black pepper, salt, cayenne, and smoked paprika. Pat the roast dry. Rub with spice mixture.

3. Heat the olive oil over medium-high heat in a Dutch oven or other large oven-safe pot until hot but not smoking. Add the roast and sear on all sides. Pour the beer and broth over the meat. Cover and roast in the oven for 3 hours or until very tender. Move the meat to a cutting board.

4. Place the Dutch oven back on the stove. Bring to a boil, stirring occasionally, until slightly reduced, about 10 minutes.

5. Shred the meat using two forks. Fill the rolls with meat and spoon a bit of sauce over the meat. Serve the remaining broth in bowls with sandwiches for dipping.

Choose the Right Brew!

A dark, rich beer just makes sense in a French dip.
Look for one with bold, roasted flavors.

Chapter 4

═ SKEWERS ═

Beer-Soaked Cantaloupe and Mozzarella Skewers . . . 43

Grilled Beer-Marinated Prosciutto-Wrapped Beef Tenderloin Skewers . . . 44

Grilled Rosemary Porter Fillet Tip Skewers . . . 45

Honey Stout Chicken Skewers . . . 47

IPA-Soaked Watermelon Skewers with Cotija and Mint . . . 48

Maple Porter–Glazed Bacon-Wrapped Dates . . . 50

Roasted Garlic Beer Butter Shrimp Skewers . . . 52

Smoky Porter Molasses Chicken Skewers . . . 53

Stout-Marinated Beef Satay with Beer Peanut Sauce . . . 57

Yogurt and Beer–Marinated Chicken Skewers . . . 58

Beer-Soaked CANTALOUPE AND MOZZARELLA SKEWERS

24 SKEWERS

1 medium cantaloupe cut in half, seeds removed

12 ounces summer ale

24 ciliegine (cherry-sized) mozzarella balls

4 large basil leaves, chopped

You're too classy to soak your fruit in beer, right? Yeah, me neither. Bring on the beer-soaked fruit—just make it fancy with a cute skewer and a hard-to-pronounce little ball of mozzarella. It's class for the beer people.

1. Using a 1" melon baller, scoop out 24 balls of cantaloupe. Place in a large bowl and cover with the ale. Refrigerate 1–3 hours.

2. Remove from the beer and skewer each melon ball along with 1 cheese ball.

3. Place on a serving plate; sprinkle with the basil.

Choose the Right Brew!

This is a perfect recipe for a mild summer ale. Look for a beer with herbal or grassy notes, and stay away from anything too high in hops . . . the beer comes through in a big way!

Grilled BEER-MARINATED PROSCIUTTO-WRAPPED BEEF TENDERLOIN SKEWERS

SERVES 8

12 ounces porter
2 tablespoons Worcestershire sauce
1 teaspoon onion powder
½ teaspoon plus 2 teaspoons kosher or sea salt, divided
1 pound beef tenderloin, cut into 1" cubes
3 ounces prosciutto

I made these for a beer event on an airfield. I was charged with beering up some food, with little more than a hibachi grill and a cooler to feed some airshow pilots. It went so well that two of the pilots nearly fought over the last skewer. Good thing I had some beer to distract the loser.

1. In a bowl or baking dish, stir together the porter, Worcestershire, onion powder, and ½ teaspoon salt.
2. Add the tenderloin cubes and marinate for 6–12 hours.
3. Preheat the grill on medium high.
4. Remove the tenderloin cubes from the marinade; discard the marinade.
5. Place the tenderloin cubes on a stack of paper towels, top with more paper towels, and allow to dry for about 10 minutes.
6. Salt the tenderloin cubes on all sides with the remaining salt.
7. Wrap the tenderloin cubes in prosciutto and thread onto metal skewers (or presoaked wooden skewers).
8. Grill on all sides until desired level of doneness, about 4 minutes per side for medium.

Choose the Right Brew!

An imperial stout or porter will work best; the meat-tenderizing properties of a high-ABV beer will make this tender steak melt in your mouth.

Grilled Rosemary PORTER
FILLET TIP SKEWERS

6–8 SERVINGS

12 ounces smoked porter
2 tablespoons Worcestershire sauce
1 teaspoon onion powder
½ teaspoon plus 2 teaspoons kosher or
    sea salt, divided
1 pound beef fillet tips
6–8 rosemary stalks, leaves removed
    from lower ¾

I'm not sure who the first guy was to stab meat with a fragrant stick and throw it onto an open flame, but I'd like to buy him a beer. Using rosemary sticks for grilling skewers is a wee bit of genius and deserving of a free beer or two. Or maybe just some hot meat.

1. In a bowl or baking dish, stir together the porter, Worcestershire, onion powder, and ½ teaspoon salt. Add the fillet tips and marinate for 6–12 hours.

2. Soak the rosemary skewers in water for 30 minutes just prior to using.

3. Preheat the grill on medium high. Remove the fillet tips from the marinade; discard the marinade.

4. Place the fillet tips on a stack of paper towels, top with more paper towels, and allow to dry for about 10 minutes.

5. Salt the fillet skewers on all sides with the remaining salt. Thread the fillet tips on the rosemary skewers.

6. Grill on all sides until desired level of doneness, about 3 minutes per side for medium. Take care when putting the skewers on the grill that the end with the rosemary leaves is off the heat and the meat end is on the grill. This will avoid setting the leaves on fire.

Choose the Right Brew!

The rich flavors of a smoked porter will lend a nice balance
to the herbal notes of the rosemary skewers.

Honey Stout CHICKEN SKEWERS

SERVES 4–6

2 cloves garlic, grated with a Microplane (or minced)

⅓ cup honey

½ cup stout

1 teaspoon red pepper flakes

½ teaspoon Dijon mustard

¼ cup soy sauce

¼ teaspoon pepper

6 boneless, skinless chicken thigh fillets, cut into bite-sized cubes

1 tablespoon olive oil

¼ cup chopped shallots (about 1 medium shallot)

Oil for the grill

Chopped cilantro for garnish

Everyone needs a great go-to tailgate recipe. When the seasons change and football games replace summer vacations, a lucky few will get to cheer the home team while wearing face paint and a parka, all while working a grill out of the back of a pickup truck. This beered-up chicken does the job and feeds the crowd. Regardless of who wins on the field, these win in the parking lot.

1. In a small bowl, whisk together the garlic, honey, stout, red pepper flakes, mustard, soy sauce, and pepper. Add the chicken cubes; refrigerate for 1 hour and up to overnight.

2. Remove the chicken from the marinade (reserve the marinade) and thread the chicken through presoaked wooden skewers.

3. In a pot over medium-high heat, add the olive oil and shallots. Sauté until the shallots have softened, about 5 minutes. Add the marinade and boil, stirring frequently, until reduced and thickened, about 8 minutes.

4. Preheat grill to medium high. Brush the grill lightly with oil. Brush the chicken with the glaze and place on the grill. Brush with glaze and turn every 2–4 minutes until cooked through, about 10 minutes. Sprinkle with chopped cilantro prior to serving.

Choose the Right Brew!

The sweetness of a milk stout is perfect for these chicken skewers. The lactose will caramelize beautifully.

IPA-SOAKED *Watermelon Skewers*
WITH COTIJA AND MINT

SERVES 8–10

1 pound watermelon, cut into 1" cubes
12 ounces IPA (plus additional as needed)
2 ounces Cotija cheese, crumbled
2 tablespoons chopped fresh mint

Soaking fruit in booze, the familiar backyard spodie, just got a massive upgrade. These delightful little cubes of beerified fruit get a classy makeover with some salty Cotija cheese and a little mint. It'll make you forget all about a red Solo cup dipped into a cooler full of booze and fruit slices.

1. Place the watermelon in a large bowl or baking dish.
2. Cover with the IPA, using just enough to fully submerge all of the watermelon.
3. Cover and refrigerate for 30 minutes, then drain.
4. Skewer each cube of watermelon with a toothpick or cocktail skewer; add to a serving plate.
5. Sprinkle with Cotija and mint. Serve chilled.

Choose the Right Brew!

Grab a beer you love; the flavor comes through in a huge way! Look for an herbal, dry-hopped IPA to lend a good balance to the salty cheese and mint.

Maple Porter–Glazed
BACON-WRAPPED DATES

MAKES 24 DATES

¹⁄₃ cup porter
½ cup real maple syrup
24 Medjool dates, pitted
3 ounces goat cheese
12 strips bacon, cut in half

It's hard to argue with bacon and beer. The natural sweetness of dates, a little creamy goat cheese, and the warmth of real maple syrup make these keepers. You might want to make a double batch.

1. Preheat oven to 400°F.

2. In a saucepan over medium-high heat, add the porter and maple syrup and boil until slightly thickened, 6–8 minutes.

3. One at a time, fill the center of each date with goat cheese, wrap with half a strip of bacon, and place on a baking sheet covered with parchment paper.

4. Brush the dates with the maple-porter mixture. Bake for 6 minutes, turn over using a pair of tongs, and brush with the maple-porter mixture. Bake for an additional 6 minutes or until the bacon is crispy.

Choose the Right Brew!

Look for a porter with a lot of rich, sweet malt flavors
to give the glaze a nice candy-like character.

Roasted Garlic BEER BUTTER SHRIMP SKEWERS

6–8 SERVINGS

1 head garlic
1 tablespoon olive oil
½ cup saison
½ cup unsalted butter, softened
2 pounds raw shrimp, deveined, shells removed
1 teaspoon salt
1 teaspoon pepper

Choose the Right Brew!

An herbal, spiced saison is a great beer for this beer butter. Look for a beer that's fairly low in hops, with nice, bold earthy notes.

This beer butter is more than just a great flavor to brush onto grilled shrimp. Save any left over for crusty bread, to add to the top of a nice steak, or to melt over some roasted vegetables. I'm not even going to look if you decide to just eat it with a spoon.

1. Preheat oven to 425°F.

2. Cut off the top point of the garlic head, keeping the bulb intact but exposing the cloves inside.

3. Place on a sheet of foil, drizzle with olive oil, and fold the foil tightly around the garlic. Place in a baking dish and roast in oven until the cloves are soft, about 20 minutes. Remove from the oven and allow to cool.

4. Add the beer to a small saucepan on the stove. Simmer until reduced to 3 tablespoons, about 10 minutes. (To lower the level of beer flavor in the butter, reduce ¼ cup of beer by half.)

5. In a food processor, add the softened butter and the beer. Squeeze the head of garlic until the cloves push out, adding just the cloves to the food processor and discarding the papery skin.

6. Process the butter until smooth; add to a small saucepan and heat until just melted. Preheat grill to medium high.

7. Skewer the shrimp with metal skewers or presoaked wooden skewers, sprinkle with salt and pepper, and brush liberally with melted butter.

8. Grill on both sides until cooked through, about 2 minutes per side. Remove from the grill and brush with melted butter.

Smoky Porter MOLASSES
CHICKEN SKEWERS

SERVES 4–6

3 cloves garlic, grated with a Microplane
(or minced)
¼ cup molasses
2 tablespoons honey
¾ cup smoked porter
1 teaspoon red pepper flakes
½ teaspoon smoked paprika
¼ cup soy sauce
1 pound boneless, skinless chicken thighs,
cut into bite-sized cubes

I'm always drawn to smoked porter. Even during a vicious mid–July heat wave, I'll order one if it's on tap. Something about the rich beer with its deep, smoky flavor has a way of reminding me why I fell in love with beer in the first place.

1. In a small bowl, whisk together the garlic, molasses, honey, smoked porter, red pepper flakes, smoked paprika, and soy sauce.

2. Add the chicken cubes, cover, and refrigerate for 2 hours and up to 8.

3. Preheat oven to 425°F. Cover a baking sheet with aluminum foil.

4. Thread the chicken onto skewers; place in an even layer on the baking sheet. Add the marinade to a pot over high heat. Cook, stirring occasionally, until reduced by about half and thickened.

5. Brush the chicken with the glaze. Bake for 10 minutes, turn over, brush with the glaze, and continue to bake until the chicken is cooked through, 8–10 additional minutes.

Choose the Right Brew!

A deep-smoked porter, especially one with notes of chilies,
will give a rich meatiness to these chicken skewers.

Stout-Marinated BEEF SATAY WITH BEER PEANUT SAUCE

SERVES 8

MARINADE
¾ cup stout
⅓ cup soy sauce
3 cloves garlic
½ teaspoon turmeric
¼ cup brown sugar
1 teaspoon red chili oil
1 clove garlic
2 pounds thin-cut skirt steak

DIPPING SAUCE
⅓ cup peanut butter
1 clove garlic
1 tablespoon lime juice
2 tablespoons soy sauce
1 teaspoon fish sauce
1 teaspoon red chili flakes
⅓ cup stout
1 tablespoon chopped shallots
1 tablespoon brown sugar

Everyone likes to eat meat off sticks. It's portable, slightly dangerous, and completely gratifying. And the sauce is so good you could drink it, although you should probably just stick to beer.

1. In a blender, add the stout, soy sauce, garlic, turmeric, brown sugar, chili oil, and garlic and blend until smooth. Place skirt steak in a bowl or baking dish and pour the marinade over the steak. Cover and chill for 1 hour.
2. Preheat grill to medium high. Remove the steak from the marinade; cut into 2" squares. Skewer with presoaked 6" wooden skewers.
3. Grill skewers to medium rare, about 2 minutes per side.
4. To make the dipping sauce, add all the dipping sauce ingredients to a blender or food processor and blend until smooth.
5. Serve the dipping sauce in a small bowl alongside the skewers.

Choose the Right Brew!

Can you get your hands on a peanut butter stout? You should grab it! It's a great beer to try and perfect for this recipe. If not, look for a creamy milk stout.

Yogurt and Beer—MARINATED
CHICKEN SKEWERS

SERVES 6–8

||||||||||||||||||||||||||||||||||||||||||||||||||||||||||

1 cup plain Greek yogurt

½ cup pale ale

1 teaspoon dried crushed red peppers

1½ teaspoons sweet smoked paprika
(or 1 teaspoon sweet and ½ teaspoon
smoked paprika)

2 tablespoons tomato paste

2 teaspoons kosher salt

1 teaspoon freshly ground black pepper

4 large cloves garlic, grated with a
Microplane

2½ pounds boneless, skinless chicken
(thighs or breast), cut into bite-sized
cubes

Vegetable oil for the grill

2 tablespoons chopped fresh parsley

Yogurt and beer give a marinade a double punch of flavor and tenderizing. The acid and sweetness of the yogurt paired with the meat-tenderizing properties of the beer make this chicken take the high heat of the grill without flinching. You'll never have dry chicken again.

1. In a large bowl, stir together the yogurt, beer, red pepper, paprika, tomato paste, salt, pepper, and garlic. Add the chicken cubes and stir until fully submerged and coated. Cover and refrigerate for at least 2 hours and up to 24.

2. Preheat grill to medium high. Remove the chicken from the marinade and thread onto metal skewers (or presoaked wood skewers); discard the marinade.

3. Brush the grill with oil to prevent sticking. Grill the chicken skewers on each side until cooked through, about 5 minutes per side.

4. Sprinkle with chopped parsley before serving.

Choose the Right Brew!

Pick a well-balanced pale ale for this, something with
a good amount of malt and some nice hops as well.

Chapter 5

CROSTINI

Beer-Braised Carnitas Crostini ... 61

Belgian Ale–Marinated Grilled Steak Crostini with IPA Chimichurri ... 63

Duck Confit Crostini with Porter Onion Jam and Pomegranates ... 65

Goat Cheese Crostini with Beer-Pickled Peaches ... 68

Porter Harissa Crostini ... 69

Parmesan Crab Beer Cheese Crostini ... 71

Peach Salsa and Beer-Battered Avocado Crostini ... 72

Smoked Salmon and Pale Ale Chive Cream Cheese Crostini ... 73

Spinach Artichoke Beer Cheese Crostini ... 75

Stout-Soaked Mushroom and Herbed Goat Cheese Crostini ... 76

Beer-Braised
CARNITAS CROSTINI

MAKES 48 CROSTINI

4-pound pork shoulder, trimmed and cut into 5" pieces
1 tablespoon kosher salt
3 tablespoons plus 2 tablespoons olive oil, divided
1 cup IPA
⅔ cup water
½ teaspoon cumin
1 teaspoon chili powder
Pinch cayenne
½ teaspoon smoked paprika
2 French baguettes, sliced into 1" slices
1 cup canned black beans
1 chipotle pepper in adobo
½ cup shredded Cheddar
½ cup shredded mozzarella
½ cup chopped tomatoes
¼ cup chopped cilantro
¼ cup Mexican crema

There is a little roadside taco stand on Sunset Boulevard in Silver Lake, California, called Burrito King. It's the real deal: no pretentiousness, no tables, no iceberg lettuce, just authentic Mexican food. The carnitas are the best thing you'll ever eat, especially after a few beers at 2 A.M. Carnitas will always bring me back to those nights, and eating carnitas with beer is just a necessity.

1. Sprinkle the salt all over the meat. Put in a shallow dish, cover, and refrigerate for 12 hours or up to 3 days.

2. Preheat oven to 325°F. In a large Dutch oven or roasting pan over 2 burners, heat the 3 tablespoons olive oil over medium-high heat until hot but not smoking. Add the meat and cook on all sides until very well browned, working in batches if necessary.

3. Remove the meat and allow to drain on a stack of paper towels. Pour the beer into the pan, scraping to deglaze the bottom; turn off heat. Add the water, cumin, chili powder, cayenne, and smoked paprika. Add the meat back in the pot. Bake uncovered until falling apart, about 3–4 hours. Pull into bite-sized pieces using a fork.

4. Preheat broiler. Lay the slices of baguette on a baking sheet in an even layer. Toast until golden brown, about 3 minutes. Flip and toast on the other side until golden brown, about 2 minutes. Lower the oven temperature to 350°F.

(continued)

5. In a food processor, add the black beans, 2 tablespoons olive oil, and chipotle pepper and process until well combined. Spread the black bean purée on one side of the toasted baguette slices.

6. Top with cheese, then carnitas; return to the oven until the cheese has melted, about 5 minutes. Remove from the oven and top with tomatoes, cilantro, and crema.

Choose the Right Brew!

A high-ABV IPA will give you a nice meat-tenderizing quality with this tough cut of meat!

Belgian ALE–MARINATED GRILLED STEAK CROSTINI WITH IPA CHIMICHURRI

MAKES 24 CROSTINI

1 pound flank steak
12 ounces Belgian ale
¼ cup Worcestershire sauce
1½ teaspoons salt, divided
1 cup Italian parsley
½ cup cilantro
¼ cup olive oil
2 tablespoons red wine vinegar
2 tablespoons IPA
2 garlic cloves
½ teaspoon crushed red chili flakes
3 tablespoons unsalted butter
1 Italian baguette, sliced into 1" slices

Of all the ways you can use beer in the kitchen, marinating a steak is a must. If I had to pick just one way to cook with beer, this would be a strong contender. Beer is a natural meat tenderizer, giving even a tough cut of meat a texture makeover.

1. Add the steak to a large bowl or baking dish. Add the Belgian ale and Worcestershire sauce.

2. Cover and refrigerate for 60 minutes. Remove from the marinade, pat dry, and sprinkle with 1 teaspoon salt.

3. Heat grill to medium high. Grill the steak on each side until medium rare, about 6 minutes per side. Remove from the grill and slice.

4. Add the parsley, cilantro, olive oil, red wine vinegar, IPA, garlic, red chili flakes, and ½ teaspoon salt to a food processor and process until smooth. Set aside.

5. Melt the butter in a pan over medium-high heat. Working in batches, add the bread and cook on each side until golden brown.

6. Top with slices of grilled steak and spoon chimichurri sauce on top.

Choose the Right Brew!

A sweet Belgian ale is a great choice for this; the malt will caramelize well on the grill.

Duck Confit CROSTINI WITH PORTER ONION JAM AND POMEGRANATES

MAKES 24 CROSTINI

FOR THE DUCK
2 duck legs
2 tablespoons kosher salt
1½ cups unsalted butter, melted
1 cup olive oil

FOR THE ONION JAM
2 tablespoons unsalted butter
2 tablespoons olive oil
2 pounds sweet white onions, sliced
⅓ cup brown sugar
12 ounces porter
¼ cup balsamic vinegar

FOR THE CROSTINI
1 Italian baguette
½ cup pomegranate seeds

Duck confit is a great option for a party. It can (and should) be made several days in advance. It sounds fancy and tastes delicious. It's an incredibly easy way to pull off Domestic Superhero—you don't even have to tell your guests how easy it was.

1. Add the duck legs to an 8" × 8" baking pan. Sprinkle with salt. Cover and chill for 24 hours.

2. Preheat oven to 275°F. Remove the duck from the pan, rinse well, and return to a clean, salt-free pan. Cover with butter and olive oil.

3. Cook at 275°F until the duck is falling off the bone, about 3 hours.

4. Cover and chill for 24 hours and up to 1 week. (Duck can be used right away, but allowing the duck to chill for at least 24 hours will allow the flavors to deepen.)

5. When ready to serve, return to a 300°F oven until the butter and olive oil is melted and the duck is warmed through. Gently shred, remove from the oil, and drain.

6. In a large pot or Dutch oven, melt 2 tablespoons butter with the olive oil over medium heat. Add the onions and sprinkle with brown sugar. Cook, stirring occasionally, until softened. Add the porter and balsamic and cook over medium-low heat, stirring occasionally, until the liquid has mostly evaporated, about 20 minutes.

7. Add the onions and any remaining liquid to a food processor and process until mostly smooth.

(continued)

8. Preheat broiler. Cut the baguette into 24 1" slices. Arrange bread slices on a baking sheet. Place under the broiler until golden brown, about 2 minutes. Flip the slices over and place back under the broiler until golden brown on the other side, about 2 minutes.

9. Spread the toast slices with onion jam, top with duck, then sprinkle with pomegranate seeds.

Choose the Right Brew!

Choose a bold, rich imperial porter for this. The onion jam needs
a big, bold beer to show up on these beautiful little bites.

Goat Cheese Crostini
WITH BEER-PICKLED PEACHES

MAKES 24 CROSTINI

¾ cup apple cider vinegar

2 tablespoons sugar

1 tablespoon salt

¾ cup pale ale

2 ice cubes (about 2–3 tablespoons water)

1 large yellow peach, sliced

3 tablespoons unsalted butter

1 sourdough baguette, cut into 1" slices

3 ounces goat cheese, softened

3 serrano chilies, thinly sliced

3 tablespoons raw honey

2 teaspoons smoked Maldon salt (a smoked, flaky sea salt)

You need to pickle some peaches. Why should cucumbers have all the fun? The sweetness of the peaches with the tart, briny tang of the pickling liquid creates a new take on America's favorite topping.

1. In a pot over medium-high heat, add the vinegar, sugar, and salt; stir until the sugar and salt have dissolved, then remove from the heat. Stir in the beer and ice cubes and allow the mixture to cool to room temperature.

2. Add the peaches to a bowl, pour the pickling liquid over the peaches, cover, and refrigerate for 1 hour and up to 3 days.

3. In a large skillet over medium-high heat, melt the butter. Add the baguette slices, cooking on each side until golden brown, about 2 minutes per side. Work in batches if necessary.

4. Spread the top side of each baguette slice with goat cheese. Top with pickled peaches and serrano chilies, then drizzle with honey and sprinkle with smoked Maldon salt.

Choose the Right Brew!
Grab a bold pale ale for these pickled peaches; look for one with earthy or herbal notes to play nice with the peaches.

Porter HARISSA CROSTINI

MAKES 24 CROSTINI

8 dried guajillo chilies (stem and seeds removed)

2 dried ancho chilies (stem and seeds removed)

1 cup room-temperature porter

1 cup warm water

3 cloves garlic, grated with a Microplane

2 tablespoons olive oil

1 tablespoon lemon juice

1 teaspoon ground coriander

½ teaspoon caraway seeds

½ teaspoon cumin

1 French baguette

1 large Haas avocado, cut into 24 slices

¼ cup chopped flat-leaf parsley

The first time I had harissa was in the middle of a traumatic day during a trip through Fez in Morocco. My guide, sensing my exhaustion, led me to the back room of a beautiful restaurant. Amidst an abundance of floor pillows and walls draped with exotic fabric, a silver plate of food was set in front of me. In a small ceramic bowl was a beautiful chili spread that I put on everything that had arrived at my table. The spicy, bold flavor gave me energy to finish the day in the old city.

1. In a small bowl, add the guajillo chilies and ancho chilies. Pour the beer and the water over the chilies. Use a heavy object such as a coffee mug to make sure the chilies are submerged. Allow to sit at room temperature for 1 hour. Drain the chilies, reserving 2 tablespoons soaking liquid.

2. Add the chilies, 2 tablespoons soaking liquid, garlic, olive oil, lemon juice, coriander, caraway, and cumin to a food processor. Process until the mixture is a paste. Harissa can be made up to 1 week ahead of time as the flavors develop over time. Make at least 1 day ahead if possible; store in the refrigerator in an airtight container until ready to use.

3. Preheat the broiler on the oven. Cut the baguette into 1" slices. Place in an even layer on a baking sheet. Place under broiler until golden brown, about 2 minutes. Flip slices over and place back under the broiler until golden brown, an additional 2 minutes.

4. Spread the harissa onto the baguette slices and top with avocado slices and chopped parsley.

(continued)

Choose the Right Brew!

A rich, dark beer is perfect for this spicy chili paste, but be aware that the higher the ABV, the hotter the final product will be. Alcohol intensifies heat; keep that in mind when selecting a beer. If you want this as spicy as it can be, grab an 18 percent barrel-aged beer!

Parmesan CRAB BEER CHEESE CROSTINI

MAKES 24 CROSTINI

1 French baguette
8 ounces cream cheese
¼ cup sour cream
1 teaspoon Old Bay Seasoning
1 teaspoon garlic powder
½ teaspoon chili powder
1 teaspoon hot pepper sauce
2 tablespoons cornstarch
⅔ cup IPA
1 tablespoon Worcestershire sauce
½ cup freshly grated Parmesan cheese
1 cup shredded mozzarella
¼ cup chopped green onions
8 ounces crab meat

Crab dip is hard to walk away from. It forces your guests to hover over the delicious dip with handfuls of chips. Which is why spreading it on portable little rounds of toast will allow for harmonious party mingling. And it frees up the other hand for a cold beer.

1. Preheat the broiler on the oven. Cut the baguette into 1" slices. Place in an even layer on a baking sheet. Place under the broiler until golden brown, about 2 minutes. Flip slices over and place back under the broiler until golden brown, an additional 2 minutes. Remove from oven; reduce temperature to 350°F.

2. In a food processor, add the cream cheese, sour cream, Old Bay, garlic powder, chili powder, hot pepper sauce, cornstarch, beer, Worcestershire sauce, Parmesan cheese, and mozzarella; process until smooth. Stir in the onions and crab meat.

3. Spoon crab mixture onto the toasted bread. Return to the oven and bake until the crab mixture has warmed, about 6 minutes.

Choose the Right Brew!

Grab a bold beer for this recipe. Look for an IPA with lots of fresh hop taste. A bold beer with notes of grass and herbs is perfect.

Peach Salsa AND BEER-BATTERED AVOCADO CROSTINI

MAKES 24 CROSTINI

1 baguette, cut into 1" slices
2 ripe but firm peaches, diced
½ cup diced red onion
2 jalapeños, diced
¼ cup chopped cilantro
Canola oil for frying
2 cups flour
½ teaspoon salt
½ teaspoon garlic powder
½ teaspoon black pepper
12 ounces IPA
3 avocados, ripe but still firm

I love peach salsa. The sweetness of the peach balances out the sharp heat of the jalapeños. Add in the creaminess of a beer–battered avocado and you might not want to share.

1. Preheat broiler. Lay the slices of baguette on a baking sheet in an even layer. Toast until golden brown, about 2 minutes. Flip and toast on the other side until golden brown, about 2 minutes.

2. Add the peaches, red onion, jalapeños, and cilantro to a small bowl and toss to combine.

3. Fill a large, heavy-bottomed saucepan with canola oil until about 3" deep. Add a deep-fry thermometer and bring the oil to about 350°F, adjusting the heat to maintain that temperature

4. In a large bowl, stir together the flour, salt, garlic powder, and pepper. Add the beer and stir until combined (should have the consistency of pancake batter).

5. Cut the avocados into thick slices (about 4 per half), making sure the skin and seed are removed.

6. Working in batches, dip the avocado slices into the batter and drop gently into the hot oil; fry until all sides are golden brown, about 3 minutes. Remove from the fryer and allow to drain on a stack of paper towels.

7. Top the bread slices with peach salsa and a slice of avocado.

Choose the Right Brew!

You want a beer with lots of carbonation for this batter. It will make for a really light and fantastic final product.

Smoked Salmon AND PALE ALE CHIVE CREAM CHEESE CROSTINI

MAKES 24 CROSTINI

8 ounces cream cheese, softened
⅓ cup pale ale
2 tablespoons chopped chives
½ teaspoon salt
1 baguette, cut into 1" slices
4 ounces smoked salmon

Some things just need to be smoked. I know what you're thinking, you little devil, but that's not the kind of smoking I mean. I've smoked pork, shrimp, corn, peaches, and even chocolate cake, but none of them lend themselves to a good smoker like a rich salmon. Even on its own, it's the star of the show. Just give it a little stage of pale ale cream cheese and watch it shine.

1. In a food processor, add the cream cheese, pale ale, chopped chives, and salt. Process until well combined.

2. Preheat broiler. Lay the slices of baguette on a baking sheet in an even layer. Toast until golden brown, about 2 minutes. Flip and toast on the other side until golden brown, about 2 minutes.

3. Spread each baguette with cream cheese. Top with a piece of smoked salmon.

Choose the Right Brew!

A well-balanced pale ale with a nice kick of hops is the perfect beer to stand up to the rich, bold smoked flavors of that salmon.

Spinach Artichoke
BEER CHEESE CROSTINI

MAKES 24 CROSTINI

1 baguette, cut into 1" slices
8 ounces cream cheese
¼ cup sour cream
3 ounces Parmesan cheese, grated (about 1 cup)
3 ounces mozzarella cheese, shredded (about 1 cup), divided in half
5 ounces frozen chopped spinach (about 1 cup), thawed and wrung dry
1 tablespoon cornstarch
½ cup IPA
1 teaspoon red chili sauce (such as sriracha)
½ teaspoon garlic powder
14 ounces quartered artichoke hearts

The thing about dips is that they tend to make people hover over the bowl with a handful of chips. There is a traffic jam around that end of the table, and party vibes are disrupted. Put that dip on a little piece of toast and call it a crostini and you have a delightful little portable dip that keeps the party moving.

1. Preheat broiler. Lay the slices of baguette on a baking sheet in an even layer. Toast until golden brown, about 2 minutes. Flip and toast on the other side until golden brown, about 2 minutes. Lower heat to 350°F.

2. In a food processor, add the cream cheese, sour cream, Parmesan, half the mozzarella, spinach, cornstarch, beer, chili sauce, and garlic powder and process until well combined.

3. Add to a saucepan over medium heat along with the artichoke hearts. Cook, stirring frequently, until hot and bubbly.

4. Spoon cheese dip onto the toasted bread and sprinkle with the remaining cheese. Return to the 350°F oven and bake until the cheese has melted, about 5 minutes. Serve warm.

Choose the Right Brew!

A bold IPA with lots of hops is the perfect beer to cut through all that cheese and sour cream.

Stout-Soaked MUSHROOM AND HERBED GOAT CHEESE CROSTINI

MAKES 18–24 CROSTINI

1 ounce (1½ cups) assorted dried mushrooms (such as porcini, shiitake, and chanterelles)

12 ounces stout

2 tablespoons unsalted butter

1 tablespoon olive oil

¼ cup chopped shallots

½ teaspoon kosher or sea salt

½ teaspoon black pepper

1 baguette (sourdough or French), cut into 1" slices

4 ounces goat cheese, softened

1 teaspoon chopped fresh thyme

1 teaspoon chopped fresh sage

1 teaspoon chopped fresh rosemary

Choose the Right Brew!

A rich, deep stout with notes of spice or coffee will add a bold taste to these mushrooms.

Nothing spans the culinary cost scale quite like the humble mushroom. From more expensive per ounce than gold to mere pennies a piece, these meaty little treats find a way into every budget. It's not hard to see why some varieties cost a small fortune—the beautiful earthy flavor is unmatched. Add the richness of a dark stout and that small fortune is more than worth it.

1. Put the mushrooms in a small bowl or jar. Cover with the stout beer. Leave at room temperature for at least 30 minutes and up to 2 hours or until the mushrooms are soft and have reconstituted.

2. Drain the mushrooms and rinse well to remove any residual grit. Cut into thin slices (unless mushrooms were presliced).

3. In a pan over medium-high heat, melt the butter with the olive oil. Add the shallots and cook until softened and starting to brown, about 5 minutes.

4. Add the mushrooms to the pan, sprinkle with salt and pepper, and cook until most of the oil and butter has been absorbed, about 5 minutes.

5. Preheat the boiler on the oven. Place the baguette slices on a baking sheet. Place under the broiler until golden brown, about 2 minutes, flip over and place under the broiler until golden brown on the opposite side, about 2 minutes.

6. In a small bowl, stir together the goat cheese, thyme, sage, and rosemary. Spread each slice with goat cheese, then top with mushrooms.

Chapter 6

= DIPS =

Beer and Bacon Dip . . . 79

Buffalo Chicken Beer Cheese Dip . . . 80

Chipotle Porter Hummus . . . 81

Crispy Shallots and Parmesan Beer Cheese Dip . . . 83

Pale Ale and Kale Tzatziki . . . 84

Parsley White Bean Beer Cheese Dip . . . 86

Porter Black Bean Dip . . . 87

Seven-Layer Jalapeño IPA Hummus Dip . . . 88

Triple-Chili Beer Cheese Dip . . . 89

Roasted Garlic and Smoked Porter Baba Ghanoush . . . 90

Beer AND BACON DIP

MAKES 3 CUPS

16 ounces cream cheese
½ cup sour cream
5 ounces mozzarella, shredded (about
    1⅔ cups)
2 ounces Cheddar, shredded
½ teaspoon smoked paprika
½ teaspoon salt
½ teaspoon chili powder
1 teaspoon garlic powder
2 tablespoons cornstarch
¾ cup IPA
8 slices bacon, cooked and chopped

It just not even fair! The rest of the dips don't even have a chance when you show up to the party with a warm, creamy dip that has both beer and bacon. You can officially take a bow and collect your prizes as King or Queen of the Dip Makers.

1. Preheat oven to 350°F.

2. Add the cream cheese, sour cream, mozzarella, Cheddar, smoked paprika, salt, chili powder, garlic powder, cornstarch, and beer to a food processor or blender.

3. Process on high until smooth and well combined, about 5 minutes. Stir in most of the chopped bacon, reserving about 2 tablespoons.

4. Pour the dip into an oven-safe bowl and top with reserved bacon. Bake until warmed through, about 15–20 minutes. Serve warm.

Choose the Right Brew!

Warm, gooey, cheesy dips need the big, bold flavors of a high-hop beer for balance. Don't be afraid of a really big IPA for this recipe.

BUFFALO CHICKEN BEER *Cheese Dip*

MAKES 3 CUPS

2 tablespoons olive oil

3 boneless, skinless chicken thighs, cut into bite-sized pieces

8 ounces sour cream

16 ounces cream cheese, softened

¾ cup grated Parmesan

¾ cup plus ½ cup shredded mozzarella, divided

⅓ cup buffalo wing sauce

⅔ cup IPA

1 teaspoon garlic powder

2 tablespoons cornstarch

½ cup blue cheese crumbles

Nothing says football watchin' like beer cheese and buffalo chicken. It just makes sense to combine the two. Add a rowdy crowd of sports fans and any dip–related altercations are not my fault, although you may want to make two bowls, just in case.

1. Preheat oven to 350°F.

2. Heat the olive oil in a large pan over medium-high heat; add the chicken and cook until browned, about 5 minutes.

3. In a food processor, add the sour cream, cream cheese, Parmesan, ¾ cup mozzarella, buffalo wing sauce, beer, garlic powder, and cornstarch; process until well combined, about 5 minutes.

4. Pour into an oven-safe dish. Stir in the chicken pieces and sprinkle with the remaining mozzarella.

5. Bake until warmed through, about 15 minutes. Remove from the oven, sprinkle with blue cheese, and serve warm with chips.

Choose the Right Brew!

There are a lot of big flavors in this dip. Grab an equally big beer to make sure those flavors come through. Have a chili IPA? That's a great choice.

Chipotle PORTER HUMMUS

SERVES 4–6

15 ounces garbanzo beans
¼ cup tahini
3 chipotle chilies in adobo sauce
3 cloves garlic
½ teaspoon cumin
3 tablespoons olive oil
3 tablespoons lemon juice
¼ cup porter

Chipotle is a beautiful flavor, and it's one of my favorites. The heat, along with the deep richness of the smoky flavor, goes well in everything from dip to braised meat. It also happens to be a great flavor for a rich, dark beer. If you haven't tried a chipotle porter, put it on your list of beers to try.

1. Add the garbanzo beans to a small bowl; rinse well. One at a time, gently pinch the beans to remove the thin, translucent skin. Discard the skin; reserve the bean.

2. Add the beans to a food processor along with the remaining ingredients and process until smooth. Serve with crudités, pita bread, or chips.

Choose the Right Brew!

A Chipotle Porter Hummus needs a chipotle porter, if you can find one. If not, look for a smoked dark porter or stout for the right kick for this recipe.

Crispy Shallots AND PARMESAN BEER CHEESE DIP

SERVES 6–8

FOR THE DIP

8 ounces cream cheese
4 ounces Parmesan, freshly grated
(about 2 cups)
1 tablespoon cornstarch
½ cup sour cream
1 teaspoon garlic powder
1 teaspoon onion powder
⅔ cup brown ale
½ teaspoon salt

FOR THE SHALLOTS

Canola oil for frying
¼ cup all-purpose flour
1 teaspoon salt
1 teaspoon black pepper
½ pound shallots, thinly sliced (about 1½
cups)

Choose the Right Brew!

A nutty brown ale is perfect, especially one with lots of hops. Look for a hoppy American brown ale to give the right kick of beer to this recipe.

Crispy shallots keep me up at night, but then again, it's not uncommon for food–related concepts to wake me from a sound sleep. After crispy shallots came into my world, I'd find myself awake at 2 A.M., writing down ideas for their uses. For instance, topping for a grilled steak, an addition to a seared ahi tuna salad, or even the perfect texture for a creamy beer cheese dip. You might want to make a double batch.

1. Preheat oven to 350°F.

2. Add the cream cheese, Parmesan, cornstarch, sour cream, garlic powder, onion powder, brown ale, and salt to a food processor. Process until smooth. Transfer to a baking dish or oven-safe serving bowl. Bake until warmed through, about 20 minutes.

3. While the dip is baking, make the shallots. Fill a large, heavy-bottomed saucepan with canola oil until about 3" deep. Add a deep-fry thermometer and bring the oil to about 250°F, adjusting the heat to maintain that temperature.

4. In a shallow bowl or large plate, stir together the flour, salt, and pepper. Working in batches, dredge the shallots in the flour mixture, then add to the hot oil; fry until golden brown. Remove with a heat-safe slotted spoon; transfer to paper towels to drain.

5. Once the dip is removed from the oven, stir and then top with crispy shallots.

Pale Ale AND KALE TZATZIKI

MAKES 3 CUPS

1 large hothouse cucumber
1 teaspoon kosher salt
16 ounces sour cream
⅓ cup pale ale
1 tablespoon lemon juice
1 tablespoon olive oil
2 cloves garlic, grated with a Microplane
2 teaspoons minced fresh dill
½ cup finely chopped kale

I'm a sucker for a clever rhyme. The kale and pale ale pairing is as fun to say as it is to eat. Of course, it tastes good, and with the addition of kale you get those nifty health benefits, but who cares! It's so fun to say!

1. Grate the cucumber and place on a stack of paper towels, then sprinkle with salt. Top with additional paper towels. Replace paper towels every 10 minutes for 30 minutes, allowing the cucumbers to drain and dry.

2. In a serving bowl, stir together the sour cream, pale ale, lemon juice, olive oil, garlic, dill, and kale. Add the cucumbers and stir until well combined.

Choose the Right Brew!

A grassy, earthy pale ale is perfect for the kale in this recipe. Look for something with moderate hops to kick the beer flavor up a notch.

Parsley White Bean
BEER CHEESE DIP

SERVES 4–6

⅓ cup chopped flat-leaf parsley
1 large clove garlic, smashed
1 ounce Parmesan, freshly grated (about ⅓ cup)
2 ounces (¼ cup) cream cheese
¼ cup IPA
1 (15-ounce) can Great Northern beans
¼ teaspoon salt
½ teaspoon black pepper

I was once presented with the task of writing an article about parsley for a food magazine. At first, I was uninspired. Parsley? How do I write 2,000 words on parsley? After a few minutes of research, I was hooked. Look at all the vitamins! And it's got calcium and iron too! But it was the bright flavor that made it a staple in my cooking. It makes a great contrast to the creamy white beans and a hoppy IPA.

1. Add all the ingredients to a food processor and process until smooth, about 4–6 minutes.

2. Add to a serving bowl. Serve with chips, bread, or crudités.

Choose the Right Brew!

A dry-hopped IPA with plenty of fresh hop flavor will be the perfect match for the parsley and creamy white beans in this recipe.

Porter BLACK BEAN DIP

MAKES 2½ CUPS

2 (15-ounce) cans black beans, rinsed
   and drained
½ cup (4 ounces) cream cheese
⅔ cup smoked porter
½ cup chopped cilantro (plus additional
   for garnish)
3 jalapeños, chopped
1 teaspoon onion powder
1 teaspoon garlic powder
½ teaspoon cumin
½ teaspoon smoked paprika
Salt and pepper to taste
¼ cup crumbled Cotija cheese

When I was a kid, bean dip came in a can with a pull tab, and I loved it. I loved the creaminess, the flavor, and the Fritos I used to scoop it out. These days, I like to update childhood favorites, and this dip is my updated version of the dip I loved. It's got more flavor, and a little beer, but it still goes pretty well with Fritos.

1. In a food processor, add the beans, cream cheese, porter, cilantro, jalapeños, onion powder, garlic powder, cumin, and smoked paprika. Process until smooth. Add salt and pepper to taste.
2. Pour into a serving bowl; top with Cotija cheese. Can be served warmed or at room temperature.

Choose the Right Brew!

You want a hoppy porter with notes of smoke
for the right balance in this dip.

Seven-Layer JALAPEÑO IPA HUMMUS DIP

SERVES 6–8

15 ounces garbanzo beans

2 fresh jalapeños, stemmed, seeded, and chopped (about ¼ cup)

3 tablespoons tahini

⅓ cup chopped cilantro

1 tablespoon olive oil

1 lime, juiced (about 1 tablespoon)

½ teaspoon garlic powder

½ teaspoon salt

⅓ cup IPA (plus additional as needed)

1 red onion, chopped

4 Persian cucumbers, chopped

1 large beefsteak tomato, chopped

½ cup kalamata olives, pitted and chopped

6 ounces marinated artichoke hearts, chopped

4 ounces feta cheese, crumbled

I was on a boat between Italy and Greece once when I wandered into the small onboard cafe to get something to eat. I ordered a Greek salad and was impressed that it wasn't what I was used to. No lettuce, and hummus instead of dressing. I was hooked. I came home and decided that delightful salad would make a pretty fantastic dip.

1. Add the garbanzo beans to a small bowl; rinse well. One at a time, gently pinch the beans to remove the thin, translucent skin. Discard the skin; reserve the bean.

2. Add the beans to a food processor along with the jalapeños, tahini, cilantro, olive oil, lime juice, garlic powder, salt, and beer. Process until smooth. Add additional IPA for a thinner dip.

3. Starting with the hummus and ending with the feta cheese, layer all the ingredients in an 8" × 8" baking dish or similar size serving dish. Serve immediately or cover and chill until ready to serve.

Choose the Right Brew!

There are a lot of flavors going on in this dip, so get a beer that can hold its own. Look for a super hoppy IPA with lots of bold flavors.

TRIPLE-CHILI BEER *Cheese Dip*

MAKES 3 CUPS

1 poblano pepper
8 ounces cream cheese
¼ cup sour cream
2½ cups shredded mozzarella
1 chipotle chili in adobo
1 jalapeño, diced
1 cup IPA
2 tablespoons cornstarch
1 teaspoon garlic powder
½ teaspoon smoked paprika
½ teaspoon salt

I've always been a bit of a heat freak. I'll always order the spiciest version of any dish on the menu, then add hot sauce. I've had to tamp down the fiery ingredients when writing recipes for mass consumption, but when it's just me and a few other capsaicin worshipers, I'll triple the power of the chilies. If you're with me on this, grab a high–ABV beer made with chilies and leave the seeds in the peppers. It's the best way to intensify the heat.

1. Move one oven rack to the top position and the second oven rack to the middle position. Preheat oven broiler.
2. Place the poblano pepper on a baking sheet. Place under broiler on the top rack until blackened, about 5 minutes. Flip over and bake on the other side until blackened. Remove from the oven and lower the oven heat to 350°F.
3. Place the poblano in a bowl, cover with plastic wrap, and steam for 10 minutes. Remove from the bowl, rub off the black skin, and remove the stem.
4. Add the poblano and remaining ingredients to a food processor. Process until smooth, then pour into a 1-quart baking dish.
5. Bake on the middle rack until warm and bubbly, about 20 minutes; serve warm.

Choose the Right Brew!

Look for a nice spicy, hoppy IPA for this dip. A pepper-spiked IPA is the best choice — this is a heat lover's beer.

Roasted Garlic AND SMOKED PORTER BABA GHANOUSH

SERVES 4–6

|||||||||||||||||||||||||||||||||||||||||||||||||||||||||||||||||||||||||||||||

2 pounds eggplant (about 2 medium-
   sized eggplants)
2 tablespoons olive oil, divided
2 teaspoons sea salt, divided
1 head garlic
3 tablespoons tahini
3 tablespoons fresh lemon juice
¼ cup smoked porter
½ teaspoon smoked paprika
¼ teaspoon chili powder
¼ teaspoon cumin

There are a lot of foods I could give up. You could not, however, take roasted garlic out of my world. I put it in dips, aioli, bread dough, and even risotto. I've even had roasted garlic ice cream. If you know someone who makes a garlic beer, send them my way; I'll be waiting.

1. Preheat oven to 425°F.

2. Cut the eggplants in half lengthwise. Brush the cut side with 1 tablespoon olive oil and sprinkle with 1 teaspoon salt. Place cut side up on a baking sheet that has been covered with aluminum foil.

3. Cut the pointed tip off the garlic, exposing all the cloves. Place on a small sheet of aluminum foil, drizzle with remaining olive oil, and close the aluminum foil tightly around the garlic. Place the garlic packet onto the baking sheet with the eggplant.

4. Roast the garlic and eggplant for 30 minutes, remove the garlic, and continue to roast the eggplant until fork tender, about 30 additional minutes. Remove the eggplant from the oven and allow to cool completely, about 1 hour.

5. Scrape out the inside of the eggplant, adding the flesh to a food processor and discarding the skin. Remove the garlic from the aluminum foil and squeeze gently until the soft cloves protrude from the head. Add the cloves to the food processer; discard the head.

6. Add the remaining ingredients, including the remaining 1 teaspoon salt, to the food processor and process until smooth. Taste, adding additional salt and lemon juice to taste.

Chapter 7

=HAND PIES,
WRAPS, & ROLLS

Beer-Brined Chicken and Strawberry Salsa Lettuce Wraps . . . 95

Beer Pesto and Beer Ricotta Mini Calzones . . . 96

Beer-Caramelized Mushroom and Spinach Hand Pies . . . 98

Blackberry Stout Wontons . . . 99

Brown Ale Pork and Apple–Filled Buns . . . 100

Chicken Beer Cheese Pretzel Empanadas . . . 102

IPA Smoked Salmon Lettuce Wraps . . . 105

Mushroom Stout Pork Hand Pies . . . 106

Smoked Stout, Caramelized Onion, and Potato Pierogies . . . 108

Tomato Beer Jam–Filled Biscuits . . . 109

Beer-Brined CHICKEN AND STRAWBERRY SALSA LETTUCE WRAPS

MAKES 10–12 LETTUCE WRAPS

1 cup brown ale
1 cup chicken broth
1 tablespoon plus 1 teaspoon kosher salt, divided
5 boneless, skinless chicken thigh fillets
½ teaspoon black pepper
3 tablespoons cornstarch
½ teaspoon chili powder
½ teaspoon brown sugar
½ teaspoon garlic powder
1 tablespoon olive oil
1 cup chopped strawberries
¼ cup small-diced red onions
¼ cup chopped cilantro
1 jalapeño, chopped, stem and seeds removed
2 tablespoons lemon juice
1 head butter lettuce
3 ounces goat cheese, crumbled

The first time I made these was after a long day of running around a strawberry field in Oxnard, California. After being so close to my food, I just wanted something fresh and bright. The sweetness of the strawberries and the creaminess of the goat cheese are a beautiful addition to a moist, beer–brined chicken.

1. Add the beer, chicken broth, and 1 tablespoon salt to a bowl and stir to combine. Add the chicken and place the bowl in the refrigerator for 3–6 hours. Remove chicken from the brine, rinse, and pat dry.

2. In a small bowl, combine the pepper, cornstarch, chili powder, 1 teaspoon salt, brown sugar, and garlic powder. Chop the chicken thighs into bite-sized pieces, removing any large pieces of fat. Toss the chicken in the spice mixture until well coated.

3. Heat the olive oil over medium-high heat until hot but not smoking. Add the chicken and sauté until cooked through, about 5–8 minutes.

4. In a small bowl, add the strawberries, red onions, cilantro, jalapeño, and lemon juice; toss to combine.

5. Fill the butter lettuce leaves with chicken, add the strawberry mixture, and top with goat cheese.

Choose the Right Brew!

A hoppy American brown ale with a high ABV (alcohol by volume) will give you a nice flavor and some great meat-tenderizing properties that are perfect for this chicken.

Beer Pesto AND BEER RICOTTA MINI CALZONES

MAKES 8 CALZONES

FOR THE RICOTTA
2 cups whole milk (do not use ultrapasteurized)
½ teaspoon salt
¼ cup plus 2 tablespoons wheat beer, divided
2 tablespoons fresh lemon juice

FOR THE PESTO
2 cloves garlic, smashed
½ cup chopped pecans
½ cup grated Parmesan
3 cups fresh basil leaves
¼ cup pale ale
⅓ cup olive oil

FOR THE CALZONES
1 pound prepared raw pizza dough
1 cup shredded mozzarella
Oil for brushing
Coarse sea salt

The first time I had homemade ricotta was in the house of a local woman in Pescara, Italy. It's hard to beat that—all other ricotta was decidedly inferior. I decided to try my hand at making it from scratch and was amazed at how simple it is. A few steps, and in about 20 minutes it was done. So of course I had to make it with beer. The nice bready flavor of a wheat beer adds a beautiful dimension to this creamy homemade cheese, even if it is missing the authenticity of eastern Italy.

1. In a pot over medium-high heat (do not use an aluminum pan), add the milk, salt, and ¼ cup wheat beer. Clip a cooking thermometer onto the side of the pan. Bring the liquid to 190°F, stirring occasionally to prevent the bottom from scorching. Keep a close eye on it; the liquid reaches and passes 190°F very quickly, and you don't want it rising above 200°F.

2. Remove from the heat, add the remaining 2 tablespoons of wheat beer and then the lemon juice, and stir gently once or twice. It should curdle immediately. Allow to sit undisturbed for about 5 minutes.

3. Line a large strainer with 1 or 2 layers of cheesecloth, and place the strainer in the sink over a large bowl. Pour the ricotta into the strainer and allow to drain for 15–30 minutes, then transfer to a bowl. (Ricotta can be made up to 3 days in advance; store in an airtight container in the refrigerator until ready to use.)

4. To make the pesto, add the garlic, pecans, Parmesan, and basil to a food processor and process until well combined. While the mixer is running, slowly add the pale ale and the olive oil until well combined. (Pesto can be made up to 1 week in advance; store in an airtight container in the refrigerator until ready to use.)

5. Preheat oven to 425°F. Cut the dough into 8 equal-sized pieces and roll each piece into a 4" circle.

6. Fill with the pesto, ricotta, and mozzarella cheese. Fold the dough over to form a crescent shape, press the edges well to seal, then transfer to a baking sheet. Brush with olive oil and sprinkle with salt.

7. Bake until golden brown, about 12 minutes.

Choose the Right Brew!

The breadiness of a wheat beer is perfect for the ricotta in this recipe. Look for a pale ale with earthy notes and a fairly low-hop profile for the pesto.

Beer-Caramelized MUSHROOM AND SPINACH HAND PIES

MAKES 9 HAND PIES

3 tablespoons unsalted butter

¼ cup chopped shallots (about 1 medium-sized shallot)

2 tablespoons olive oil

2 cups chopped cremini mushrooms

½ cup dark Belgian ale

4 cups fresh baby spinach leaves, lightly packed

3 ounces goat cheese

¼ cup fresh-grated Parmesan

1 sheet puff pastry

2 tablespoons melted unsalted butter

I was never a huge spinach fan until I had it sautéed with mushrooms. There is something about the earthiness of these two vegetables that just works; they complement and contrast each other in flavor and color. After that, it just seemed like I couldn't have one without missing the other. So wrap them both up in some flaky puff pastry and all is right in the world.

1. Preheat oven to 400°F.

2. In a pan over medium-high heat, melt the butter. Add the shallots and cook until softened, about 5 minutes.

3. Add the olive oil and mushrooms. Cook until the mushrooms have darkened, about 5 minutes. Lower the heat to medium, add the beer, and cook until the beer is gone and the pan is mostly dry, about 8 minutes.

4. Add the spinach and stir until the spinach has darkened and wilted, about 3 minutes.

5. Turn off the heat; stir in the goat cheese and Parmesan.

6. Roll out the puff pastry on a lightly floured surface. Cut into 9 (3") squares.

7. Add 2–3 tablespoons of filling to the center of each square. Moisten the edges with water, fold over, and press to seal well.

8. Transfer to a baking sheet; poke 1 or 2 small slits in the top of each hand pie. Brush with melted butter. Bake until golden brown, about 12 minutes.

Choose the Right Brew!

A malty, sweet Belgian ale is perfect to balance out the earthiness of the mushrooms in this recipe.

Blackberry Stout WONTONS

MAKES 24 WONTONS

1 pound blackberries (fresh or frozen)
1½ cups powdered sugar plus ¼ cup for
   dusting
1 cup stout
½ teaspoon salt
2 tablespoons cornstarch
24 wonton wrappers
Oil for frying

In Seattle, blackberries grow like weeds—although they are the most delicious weeds I've ever come across. When the later summer months present me with an abundance of these delicious little berries, I need to get creative. Stout lends itself well to the sweet fruitiness of the blackberries, and no one is ever mad about anything being deep-fried.

1. In a pot over medium-high heat, stir together the blackberries, 1½ cups sugar, beer, salt and cornstarch. Bring to a simmer and stir until very thick, about 10 minutes (frozen berries will take longer). Allow to cool to room temperate, about 20 minutes.

2. Place a small bowl of water on a flat work surface. One at a time, place a wonton wrapper on the work station and add 1 tablespoon filling to the center. Moisten the edges with water (use either your fingers or a pastry brush) and fold the wrapper over, forming a triangle; press well to seal. Fold 2 corners in toward the center, using water to secure in place. Repeat for all wrappers.

3. Add 4" of oil to a saucepan with a deep-fry thermometer clipped to the side; adjust the heat to maintain 350°F.

4. Two at a time, fry the wontons until golden brown, about 1 minute per side. Transfer to a stack of paper towels to drain. Sprinkle with the remaining powdered sugar and serve warm.

Choose the Right Brew!

A slightly sweet, rich stout is perfect for this recipe. Look for a chocolate stout or a milk stout to give the right kick to these blackberries.

Brown Ale PORK AND APPLE–FILLED BUNS

MAKES 12 BUNS

3 cups flour

2¼ teaspoons (1 envelope) rapid-rise yeast

2 teaspoons sugar

1 cup wheat beer or pale ale

½ teaspoon salt

3 tablespoons oil

2 tablespoons unsalted butter

1 cup chopped white onions

1 Granny Smith apple, peeled and chopped (about 1 cup)

1 pound ground pork

½ cup brown ale

1 teaspoon chopped fresh sage

½ cup freshly grated Parmesan cheese

Egg wash (1 egg and 1 tablespoon water beaten together)

Brown ale is one of my favorite pairings with a mild white meat like pork. The rich nuttiness brings out the meatiness without being overbearing. It has a way of highlighting and complementing rather than detracting. The brown ale also works well with the sweet–tart bite of an apple.

1. In the bowl of a stand mixer fitted with a dough hook attachment, add the flour, yeast, and sugar. Mix until combined.

2. In a microwave-safe bowl, add the beer. Microwave on high for 20 seconds, test the temperature with a cooking thermometer, and repeat until the temperature reaches 120°F–125°F.

3. Add the beer to the stand mixer bowl and mix on medium speed. Once most of the dough has been moistened, sprinkle with the salt and drizzle in the oil while the mixer is still running.

4. Turn speed to high and beat until the dough is smooth and elastic, about 8 minutes. Transfer the dough to a lightly oiled bowl and tightly wrap with plastic wrap. Allow to sit in a warm room until doubled in size, about 45–60 minutes.

5. Remove from the bowl and add to a lightly floured surface. Knead several times, then cut into 12 equal-sized pieces.

6. While the dough is rising, make the filling. Preheat oven to 350°F. Melt the butter in a pan over medium-high heat; add the onions and the apples and cook until softened, about 8 minutes.

7. Add the pork and cook until just starting to brown but not cooked through. Add the brown ale and simmer until the beer is mostly gone and the pork is cooked through, about 10 minutes. Stir in the sage and cook for about 2 minutes. Remove from the heat and stir in the cheese.

8. One at a time, roll the dough into 6" circles. Add about ¼ cup filling to the center and form into a tight circle around the filling. Place on a baking sheet, seam side down. Brush with egg wash. Bake until golden brown, 12–15 minutes.

Choose the Right Brew!

Look for a nutty brown ale to give the pork the right balance.

Chicken Beer Cheese
PRETZEL EMPANADAS

MAKES 8 EMPANADAS

FOR THE CRUST
2½ cups flour
1 tablespoon sugar
½ teaspoon garlic powder
1 envelope (2¼ teaspoons) rapid-rise
  yeast
1 cup wheat beer
1 teaspoon kosher salt
2 tablespoons oil
10 cups water
¼ cup baking soda
1 large egg lightly beaten
1 tablespoon coarse salt

FOR THE FILLING
1 pound boneless skinless chicken thighs,
  cut into bite-sized cubes
½ teaspoon salt
1 teaspoon onion powder
1 teaspoon garlic powder
1 tablespoon olive oil
4 ounces sharp Cheddar cheese, shredded
  (1¾ cups)
1 tablespoon cornstarch
3 tablespoons sour cream
¼ cup IPA

Beer and pretzels have always had a furious love affair. The salty pretzels and the cold carbonation of the beer could teach a master class in harmonious food pairings. So it's going to be no surprise that beer–stuffed pretzels are fairly mind–blowing.

1. Add the flour, sugar, garlic powder, and yeast to the bowl of a stand mixer fitted with a dough hook attachment. Stir to combine.

2. In a microwave-safe bowl, add the beer. Microwave for 20 seconds, test the temperature, and repeat until the beer reaches 120°F.

3. Pour the beer into the flour mixture and stir at a low speed until most of the dough has been moistened. Add the kosher salt and oil, turn the speed up to high, and mix until the dough gathers around the hook and is smooth, about 8 minutes.

4. Oil a large bowl with olive oil. Remove the dough from the mixer, form into a ball, and place in prepared bowl; then cover tightly with plastic wrap. Allow to sit in a warm, dry area until doubled in size, about 40–60 minutes.

5. Remove the dough from the bowl and knead on a lightly floured surface until smooth, about 2 minutes. Cut into 8 equal-sized pieces. Preheat oven to 375°F.

6. Sprinkle the chicken on all sides with salt, onion powder, and garlic powder. Heat the olive oil in a skillet over medium-high heat. Cook the chicken until browned, about 8 minutes.

7. In a food processor or blender, add the cheese, cornstarch, sour cream, and IPA; blend until smooth. Pour over the chicken, then simmer until thickened. Remove from the heat.

8. One at a time, roll the dough pieces out on a lightly floured surface into 6" circles. Fill each with about 3 tablespoons of the chicken mixture. Fold the dough over the filling, making crescent shapes, and roll the edges together, pressing with a fork to seal well. Add to a baking sheet covered with parchment paper.

9. Fill a large pot with 10 cups water, making sure there is room for it to bubble up without spilling over but deep enough for the pretzels. Bring the water to a boil, then add the baking soda. One at a time, gently place each pretzel into the boiling baking soda water and cook, turning once, for about 30 seconds. Remove from the water with a slotted spatula and place back on the baking sheet; allow to dry.

10. Brush liberally with the beaten egg and sprinkle with salt. Bake for 20 minutes or until dark golden brown in color.

Choose the Right Brew!

The sharp Cheddar in this recipe balances nicely with a high-hop IPA that has a strong malt backbone. The pretzel dough works well with a bready wheat beer.

IPA SMOKED SALMON *Lettuce Wraps*

MAKES 2 CUPS

8 ounces cream cheese, softened
¼ cup sour cream
3 tablespoons IPA
½ teaspoon salt
¼ teaspoon cayenne pepper
4 ounces smoked salmon, chopped
¼ cup chopped chives
4 large heads endive, separated into leaves

Endive leaves make delightful little delivery vehicles for a creamy dip. A nice cold crunch to go with a rich, smoky salmon dip feels perfect. Be sure not to make these too far in advance or the leaves will get soggy and you'll lose that lovely crispy snap.

1. Add the cream cheese, sour cream, beer, salt, and cayenne pepper to a food processor; process until well combined.

2. Add the salmon and chives; pulse until combined.

3. Add to a piping bag (or large plastic storage bag with one corner tip cut off) and pipe into the endive leaves. Chill until ready to serve, taking care not to make too far in advance to avoid the leaves becoming soggy.

Choose the Right Brew!

It's best to use a smoked IPA in this recipe. However, if you can't get ahold of one, a malty IPA works just as well.

Mushroom Stout
PORK HAND PIES

MAKES 8–10 HAND PIES

FOR THE DOUGH
2¼ cups flour, divided
1 teaspoon salt
10 tablespoons unsalted butter, cold, cut into cubes
1 large egg
⅓ cup cold pale ale
¼ cup melted unsalted butter
Pinch salt

FOR THE FILLING
2 tablespoons olive oil (plus more as needed)
¼ cup chopped onions
2 cloves garlic, minced
½ cup chopped cremini or white button mushrooms
1 pound ground pork
½ cup stout
1 cup chopped tomatoes
½ cup chopped roasted red bell peppers
1 teaspoon salt
½ teaspoon pepper
1 teaspoon smoked paprika
1 teaspoon chili powder

It just makes sense. Take something as beloved as a pie, make it smaller, and wrap it up in a portable little package, and people are just going to be happy. It's savory, a pie dynamic we all should indulge in more often, and it's easy to hold in one hand. Freeing up your other hand for a beer.

1. Put 1½ cups flour and the salt in a food processor and pulse to combine. Add the butter and process until combined. Add the remaining flour and process again. Move to a bowl. In a small bowl, beat the egg and beer together until well combined, then add the egg mixture to the dough and mix with a wooden spoon. Form into a disk, cover with plastic wrap, and chill for at least 1 hour.

2. Heat the oil in a saucepan over medium heat. Add the onions and cook until softened, about 3 minutes. Add the garlic and the mushrooms and cook until the mushrooms are soft, adding a little more oil if the pan gets dry. Add the pork and cook until browned but not completely cooked through, about 5 minutes. Add the stout and cook until reduced by half, about 6 minutes. Add the remaining filling ingredients and cook until warm and combined, about 3 minutes. Allow to cool.

3. Preheat oven to 400°F. Once the dough is chilled, roll out on a flat surface and cut into sections that are 6" × 8". Add ¼ cup of the filling to one end of the strip, keeping at least 1" between the filling and the edges. Fold the empty half over the filling and press the edges until secure.

4. Transfer to a baking sheet (sprayed with cooking spray or covered with parchment paper to prevent sticking). Brush the tops of the pies with melted butter and sprinkle with a little salt. Bake for 20–25 minutes or until golden brown.

Choose the Right Brew!

For the dough, grab a pale ale, or even a pale lager, with lots of carbonation. It'll give you a nice light texture. For the filling, look for a stout with notes of coffee or pepper to add the right flavors to the pork.

Smoked Stout, CARAMELIZED ONION, AND POTATO PIEROGIES

MAKES 24 PIEROGIES

1½ cups flour
½ teaspoon salt
2 large eggs
¼ cup pale ale
1 pound russet potatoes, peeled and chopped
3 tablespoons unsalted butter
1 cup chopped sweet white onions
1 tablespoon olive oil plus 2 tablespoons for frying
½ cup smoked stout

Choose the Right Brew!

A smoked porter or stout will give a big, bold, meaty flavor to those onions. Look for one with moderate hops and a nice amount of malt as well.

If there is one thing that makes a meal feel like comfort food, it's potatoes. And caramelized onions. And beer. So it's great that this has all three. Comfort food level: expert.

1. In a small bowl, stir together the flour and salt, then make a well in the center. Add the eggs and beer. Stir together into a dough ball. Knead on a lightly floured surface until smooth and elastic. Cover and allow to rest at room temperature for 30 minutes.

2. While the dough rests, make the filling. Cook the potatoes in lightly salted boiling water until fork tender; drain.

3. In a pan over medium heat, melt the butter. Add the onions and olive oil and cook until the onions have softened, about 5 minutes. Add the stout and cook, stirring occasionally, until the beer has evaporated and the onions have caramelized, about 15 minutes.

4. Add the potatoes, mashing and stirring until well combined. Remove from the heat.

5. Divide the dough into 24 small balls. Roll each ball into a flat circle. Fill with about 1 tablespoon of filling, folding over the dough and pressing to seal well.

6. Working in batches, cook the pierogies in lightly salted boiling water until tender, about 10 minutes.

7. Heat 2 tablespoons olive oil in a pan over medium-high heat. Add the boiled pierogies and cook until browned on the bottom.

Tomato Beer
JAM-FILLED BISCUITS

MAKES 10 BISCUITS

FOR THE FILLING
2 tablespoons olive oil
1 medium shallot, sliced (about ⅓ cup)
2 cups grape tomatoes (about ¾ pound)
⅔ cup Belgian ale
1 tablespoon brown sugar
2 teaspoons balsamic vinegar
½ teaspoon black pepper
½ teaspoon chopped fresh rosemary, divided
⅓ cup freshly grated Parmesan

FOR THE BISCUITS
5¼ cups all-purpose flour
1 tablespoon baking powder
2 teaspoons baking soda
1 teaspoon salt
2 teaspoons sugar
12 tablespoons unsalted cold butter, cut into cubes
¾ cup buttermilk
1 cup Belgian ale (or wheat beer)
3 tablespoons melted unsalted butter
½ teaspoon coarse sea salt

I was once on a horrible TV show trying to hock beer-flavored jam. It was terrible; the editing made me look sad and ill-informed. The last day of shooting, at nearly 3 A.M., I was asked why the jam wasn't sweet. I tried, in vain, to explain that not all jam is sweet. Plenty of jam is savory—in fact, some of the best jam is savory. Unfortunately, that was deleted in favor of a shot of me staring blankly into space. Although I'm no longer a fan of reality TV, I'll always be a fan of savory jam.

1. Preheat oven to 400°F.

2. Heat the olive oil in a pot over medium-high heat; add the shallots and cook until softened, about 5 minutes. Add the tomatoes and cook until blistered. Add the beer, brown sugar, balsamic, black pepper, and ¼ teaspoon rosemary. Reduce heat to maintain a simmer. Simmer until thickened and tomatoes have broken down, about 20 minutes.

3. In a food processor, add the flour, baking powder, baking soda, salt, sugar, and remaining ¼ teaspoon rosemary. Pulse to combine. Add the cold butter and process until well combined.

4. Add the buttermilk and beer. Mix with a fork until just combined.

5. Add to a well-floured flat surface, then pat into a rectangle. Using a cold rolling pin (preferably marble), gently roll into a large rectangle about 1" thick, using as few strokes as possible. Fold the dough into thirds as you would a letter about to go into an envelope. Roll lightly once in each direction to about 1" thickness; fold in thirds again. Gently roll to about 1½" thickness

(continued)

6. Using a 2" biscuit cutter, cut out 20 circles. Place 10 circles on a baking sheet; spoon jam into the center of each circle. Top each circle with another biscuit circle, pressing to seal.

7. Brush the tops with melted butter and sprinkle with salt. Bake until golden brown, about 12 minutes.

Choose the Right Brew!

The acidity of a tomato is balanced out nicely by a nice malty Belgian ale. Look for a sweet and slightly spiced Belgian to round this out.

Chapter 8

HANDFULS: NUTS, OLIVES, POPCORN

Beer and Sriracha–Candied Nuts . . . 113

Beer-Battered Gorgonzola-Stuffed Olives . . . 115

Beer-Candied Pecans . . . 116

Beer Sausage–Stuffed Crispy Fried Olives . . . 117

Chili Lime Beer Roasted Peanuts . . . 118

Chocolate and Stout–Coated Almonds . . . 119

Curried Belgian Ale Mixed Nuts . . . 121

Cocoa and Stout Roasted Almonds . . . 122

Garlic Beer–Butter Popcorn . . . 123

Salted Beer Caramel Corn . . . 124

Beer and SRIRACHA–CANDIED NUTS

MAKES 2½ CUPS

⅓ cup IPA
½ cup brown sugar
1 tablespoon unsalted butter
¼ teaspoon sriracha
Pinch cayenne
2½ cups mixed nuts

If I'm ever the proud owner of a beer bar, I'll serve up some candied nuts. Not just any candied nuts, but ones that make you want another sip of that beer you ordered. Sure, those nuts will be free, and they'll be so good that you'll eat them by the handful, but that perfect mix of sweet, salty, and spicy will make you want more beer. Which you'll have to pay for. I'm pretty devious.

1. Preheat oven to 350°F.

2. Add the beer and brown sugar to a large saucepan over medium heat. Stir until the sugar has melted. Bring to a boil and allow to boil untouched for 3 minutes.

3. Remove from the heat; stir in the butter, sriracha, and cayenne. Add the nuts and stir until all the nuts are well coated.

4. Line a baking sheet with a silicone baking mat (or parchment paper) and spread nuts in an even layer on prepared baking sheet.

5. Bake for 6 minutes, stir, then bake for an additional 6 minutes. Remove from the oven, allow to cool, then break apart.

Choose the Right Brew!

Can you get your hands on a smoked IPA? Great, go with that. If not, look for a malty IPA to do the job.

Beer-Battered GORGONZOLA-STUFFED OLIVES

SERVES 4–6

1 cup Spanish olives (remove pimento if necessary)
1 ounce Gorgonzola cheese
1 cup all-purpose flour
2 tablespoons cornstarch
1 tablespoon baking powder
Pinch salt
1 cup wheat beer
Canola oil for frying

Leave me alone with a jar of olives and it'll disappear faster than my beer. So it doesn't even seem fair that I've stuffed them with a tangy cheese and battered and fried them. I'm powerless.

1. One at a time, stuff the olives with Gorgonzola cheese and place on a wire rack over a baking sheet.

2. In a small bowl, stir together the flour, cornstarch, baking powder, and salt. Stir in the beer until well combined.

3. Heat 3" of oil in a pot over medium-high heat. Use a deep-fry thermometer to bring the oil to 350°F, adjusting the heat to maintain that temperature.

4. Working in batches of 2 or 3 at a time, dip the olives in the batter, lift with a fork to allow excess batter to drip off, add to the oil, and fry until golden brown on all sides, about 1 minute total.

5. Return to the wire rack and allow to cool before serving.

Choose the Right Brew!

The breadiness a wheat beer is perfect for a nice beer batter. Look for something with lots of carbonation to give you a nice lightness to your batter.

BEER-CANDIED *Pecans*

MAKES 2¼ CUPS

½ cup black IPA
1 cup golden brown sugar, packed
1 tablespoon unsalted butter
½ teaspoon salt
2 cups pecan halves

These sweet and salty little handfuls of flavorful pecans are just as addictive as any candy I've ever some across. But they're nuts, which have protein, so they're not bad for you. It's totally okay to eat the entire batch, right? Right?

1. Preheat oven to 250°F.

2. In a pot over high heat, add the beer and brown sugar. Stir until the sugar has dissolved.

3. Clip a candy thermometer on the side of the pan. Bring the liquid to 235°F, then remove from the heat.

4. Add the butter; stir until combined.

5. Add the salt and pecans; stir until the pecans have all been coated.

6. Pour the pecans onto a baking sheet that has been covered with a silicone baking mat (or aluminum foil that has been sprayed with cooking spray). Spread evenly over the sheet.

7. Bake for 15 minutes, stir, and bake for an additional 15 minutes (if the pecans look foamy, stir until the bubbles have dissolved).

8. Allow to cool to room temperature, then break apart.

Choose the Right Brew!

A black IPA gives the right balance of hops and malt, with the addition of a gorgeous dark color that's perfect for this recipe.

Beer Sausage–Stuffed
CRISPY FRIED OLIVES

MAKES 40 OLIVES

½ pound raw Italian sausage (removed from casings)
2 tablespoons plus ⅓ cup pale ale, divided
1 teaspoon red pepper flakes
1 large egg
⅓ cup flour
½ cup Italian bread crumbs
Canola oil for frying
40 pitted black olives

I'm not going to lie to you—these take some work. There is the sausage to stuff in the olives, there is hot, unruly oil to contend with, there is beer batter to get all over the kitchen. But they are also delicious, the talk of the party even. They are a lot of work, but they'll pull their weight once they're made.

1. In a small bowl, stir together the sausage, 2 tablespoons pale ale, and red pepper flakes.

2. In a separate bowl, whisk together the egg and ⅓ cup pale ale. In a separate bowl or plate, add the flour. In a separate bowl or plate, add the bread crumbs.

3. Fill a large, heavy-bottomed saucepan with canola oil until about 3" deep. Add a deep-fry thermometer and bring the oil to 350°F, adjusting the heat to maintain that temperature.

4. Stuff the olives with sausage, roll in flour, coat in egg wash, and then roll in bread crumbs.

5. A few at a time, fry until golden brown and the sausage is cooked, about 3 minutes. Remove from the oil and allow to drain on a wire rack.

Choose the Right Brew!

Use the same pale ale for the sausage as well as the beer batter. To make both elements hoppy, look for a well-carbonated pale ale with a nice bit of spice or herbs.

Chili Lime Beer ROASTED PEANUTS

MAKES 2 CUPS

¼ cup IPA
2 tablespoons chili powder
½ teaspoon smoked paprika
¼ teaspoon cayenne pepper
1 teaspoon salt
1 tablespoon honey
2 tablespoons lime juice
2 cups unsalted peanuts (shelled)

Chili and lime are a lot like hops and malt: It's all about balance. The warmth of the chili is always balanced so beautifully by the coolness of the lime. Plus, you get to add beer, which is always fun.

1. Preheat oven to 400°F.

2. In a pot over medium-high heat, add the beer, chili powder, smoked paprika, cayenne, salt, honey, and lime and bring to a low simmer. Simmer until thickened, about 3 minutes.

3. Remove from the heat and stir in the peanuts until well coated. Pour in an even layer on a baking sheet that has been covered with a silicone baking mat or parchment paper.

4. Bake until dried, about 8 minutes.

Choose the Right Brew!

Look for a citrusy IPA with plenty of hops to give
you the right notes for these nuts.

Chocolate AND
STOUT–COATED ALMONDS

MAKES 2½ CUPS

⅓ cup stout
4 ounces dark chocolate (60 percent
    cocoa content)
2 cups almonds
¼ cup unsweetened cocoa powder
¼ cup powdered sugar

When Christmas rolls around I like to make dozens and dozens of homemade, chocolate-coated, beer-infused treats—mostly because of the reaction they get. People adore chocolate, and it goes well with a deep stout.

1. Add the beer to a pot over high heat. Reduce by half, stirring frequently. Remove from the heat, add the chocolate, and stir until smooth and melted.

2. Add the almonds and stir until well coated, remove with a fork, and add to a plate or baking sheet covered with parchment paper. Chill until the chocolate has set, about 1 hour.

3. In a small bowl, stir together the cocoa powder and powdered sugar. Roll the almonds in the cocoa-sugar mixture until well coated.

Choose the Right Brew!

A rich, deep imperial stout will hit the right note
with these chocolate-covered almonds.

Curried Belgian ALE MIXED NUTS

MAKES 2 CUPS

1 tablespoon unsalted butter
2 tablespoons brown sugar
¼ cup Belgian ale
1 teaspoon garlic powder
1 teaspoon kosher salt
1 teaspoon curry powder
Pinch cayenne
¼ teaspoon chili powder
1 pound mixed nuts

There has always been something exotic and seductive about curry. The heat, the spice, the warmth, the images of foreign open–air markets and large colorful platters of coconut–drenched meats. These are a small handful of those great flavors for your party.

1. Preheat oven to 250°F.

2. In a saucepan over medium-high heat, melt the butter with the brown sugar and beer. Boil until slightly thickened, about 6 minutes.

3. Turn off the heat and add the garlic powder, salt, curry powder, cayenne, and chili powder; stir to combine. Add the nuts; toss to coat.

4. Add the nuts to a baking sheet lined with a silicone mat or parchment paper. Bake for 15 minutes. Stir the nuts, then bake for an additional 15 minutes.

5. Allow to cool completely, break apart, then transfer to an airtight container to store.

Choose the Right Brew!

The strong flavors of curry get a nice balance from a Belgian ale. Grab one that's malty and has some spice notes like cloves or cinnamon.

Cocoa AND STOUT ROASTED ALMONDS

MAKES 2 CUPS

¼ cup chocolate stout
½ cup sugar
2 tablespoons cocoa powder
1 tablespoon cornstarch
2 cups almonds
½ teaspoon coarse sea salt

The rich flavor of cocoa powder lends itself well to roasted almonds with a malty chocolate stout to hold it all together. Try finishing these with a little smoked salt or even a chili salt to mix things up a bit.

1. Preheat oven to 375°F.

2. In a pot over medium-high heat, add the beer, sugar, cocoa powder, and cornstarch. Stir until thickened, about 5 minutes.

3. Remove from the heat, add the almonds, and stir until coated.

4. Pour onto a baking sheet that has been lined with a silicone baking mat or parchment paper, and spread into an even layer. Sprinkle with salt.

5. Bake for 10 minutes, remove from the oven, and allow to cool before breaking apart.

Choose the Right Brew!

A rich, chocolaty stout is the right beer for this job.

GARLIC BEER–BUTTER *Popcorn*

MAKES 4 CUPS

2 tablespoons canola or grapeseed oil
½ cup popcorn kernels
3 tablespoons unsalted butter, melted
2 tablespoons pale ale
½ teaspoon garlic powder
½ teaspoon kosher salt

This is the perfect snack for a movie night. Maybe a beer–themed movie party? Or maybe just an old favorite, some great beer, and some beer–buttered popcorn to make movie night a special occasion.

1. Add the oil to a pot with a lid, add a few kernels, cover, and put on high heat. Once the corn starts popping, add the remaining corn kernels and cover tightly.

2. Once the corn starts popping rapidly, remove from the heat, keeping the pot tightly covered until the popping stops.

3. In a small bowl, combine the melted butter, pale ale, garlic powder, and salt. Drizzle over the popcorn, tossing to coat.

Choose the Right Brew!

A pale ale with medium hops, a bit of malt, and some citrus notes balance out the rich butter and garlic flavors.

Salted Beer CARAMEL CORN

MAKES 7¼ CUPS

7 cups plain popped corn
⅔ cup brown sugar
2 tablespoons light corn syrup
½ cup plus 2 tablespoons imperial stout, divided
4 tablespoons unsalted butter
1 teaspoon coarse sea salt

Homemade caramel corn is the perfect fall party food. The marriage of sweet and salty, with an addictive crunch, keeps you coming back for more. It also just so happens to pair wonderfully with a Belgian dubbel ale.

1. Preheat oven to 250°F.
2. Spray a large baking pan with cooking spray. Add the popcorn to the baking sheet in an even layer and place in the oven until the caramel sauce is ready.
3. Add the brown sugar, light corn syrup, ½ cup stout, and butter to a saucepan over high heat. Stir until the sugar dissolves, then stop stirring. Allow to boil for 7 minutes, without stirring. Remove from the heat and immediately stir in the remaining 2 tablespoons stout.
4. Spray a silicone spatula with cooking spray (except the handle). Gently pour the caramel sauce over the corn, stirring with the spatula to coat.
5. Bake for 20 minutes, stir, and bake for an additional 20 minutes. Remove from the oven and spread evenly onto a sheet of parchment or wax paper; sprinkle immediately with salt. Allow to cool until hardened. Store in an airtight container.

Choose the Right Brew!

This needs a big, huge stout. Look for an imperial stout or porter to give you some beer notes in the final product.

Chapter 9

TARTLETS
AND MINI PIES

Beer-Braised Lamb Shank Tarts with Belgian Cherry Sauce ... 127

Goat Cheese and Bacon Tarts with Pale Ale Polenta Crust ... 130

Belgian Ale–Caramelized Apple and Onion Tarts ... 131

Belgian Ale Ricotta Tarts with Roasted Figs and
Honey Beer Caramel Sauce ... 134

Blackened Beer-Brined Chicken Masa Tarts with IPA Guacamole ... 138

Grilled Barbecue Chicken and Peach Mini Pizzas ... 140

Grilled Brie and Prosciutto Flatbreads with Honey-Orange Beer Glaze ... 142

Hoisin Stout–Braised Pork Rib Tarts ... 145

Beer–Caramelized Mushroom Gorgonzola Tart ... 146

Porter-Soaked Plum, Bacon, and Arugula Tarts ... 147

Beer-Braised LAMB SHANK TARTS
WITH BELGIAN CHERRY SAUCE

MAKES 12–14 TARTS

FOR THE TART DOUGH
1¼ cups all-purpose flour, divided
½ teaspoon salt
1 tablespoon sugar
10 tablespoons unsalted butter
3 tablespoons ice-cold pale ale

FOR THE LAMB
2 lamb shanks
½ teaspoon salt
½ teaspoon pepper
3 tablespoons olive oil
3 tablespoons unsalted butter
1 cup chopped white onions
¼ cup brown sugar
12 ounces stout

FOR THE BELGIAN CHERRY SAUCE
2 tablespoons unsalted butter
¼ cup chopped shallots
2 cups (9 ounces) fresh Bing cherries, pitted
12 ounces Belgian ale
½ teaspoon salt
1 teaspoon black pepper
¼ cup chopped Italian parsley

If you want to look like an episode of Dexter, skip the apron when you're pitting cherries. Me, it's the only time I wear one. Most of the time I have a kitchen towel tucked into my back pocket, within grabbing distance to wipe hands and spills, but when I pit cherries, I suit up. You should too, unless, of course, red splatter stains are your sort of thing.

1. Add ¾ cup flour, salt, and sugar to a food processor; pulse to combine. Add the butter and process until well combined and dough gathers around the blade.

2. Add the remaining flour and pulse 6–8 times or until all the flour has been coated.

3. Transfer to a bowl. Using a rubber spatula or wooden spoon, stir in the beer until completely incorporated into the dough. Dough will be very soft.

4. Lay a long sheet of plastic wrap on a flat surface. Add the dough and form into a disk. Refrigerate until chilled, about 1 hour and up to 3 days.

5. Sprinkle the lamb shanks on all sides with salt and pepper.

6. In a large saucepan, heat the olive oil over medium-high heat until very hot. Add the lamb, sear on all sides until golden brown, then remove from the pot; set aside.

7. Add the butter and onions and cook until the onions have started to soften, about 5 minutes. Reduce heat to medium, add the sugar and stout, and scrape to deglaze the pan. Add the lamb back into the pot. Add the lid at a vent, adjusting heat to maintain a low simmer; do not boil.

(continued)

8. Cook until the lamb is fork tender, about 2 hours. Using two forks, shred lamb into bite-sized pieces.

9. While the lamb is cooking, make the cherry sauce. Heat the butter in a pot over medium-high heat; add the shallots and cook until softened, about 5 minutes. Add the cherries, Belgian ale, salt, and pepper. Simmer until thickened and cherries have broken down, about 15 minutes.

10. Preheat oven to 350°F. Roll the dough out on a lightly floured surface. Using a biscuit cutter, cut out 12–14 circles, about 3" in diameter. Place on a baking sheet; prick with a fork several times.

11. Bake until golden brown, about 15 minutes. Top each tart crust circle with lamb and a drizzle of cherry sauce. Sprinkle with parsley.

Choose the Right Brew!

With three beers for one recipe, you better like what you're opening because you'll have plenty left over for drinking. Choose a pale ale with nice carbonation for the crust, a stout with coffee or cocoa notes for the lamb, and a malty Belgian for the cherries.

Goat Cheese AND BACON TARTS WITH PALE ALE POLENTA CRUST

MAKES 12 TARTS

2 tablespoons unsalted butter
1 cup pale ale
1 cup heavy cream
½ cup corn grits
½ teaspoon salt
2 ounces crumbled goat cheese
4 strips bacon, cooked and crumbled
3 tablespoons chopped green onions

Polenta is a great showcase for a pale ale. The flavor comes across in a subtle but beautiful way, and the residual hops are balanced nicely by the creamy goat cheese and the mild sweetness of the bacon.

1. Preheat oven to 375°F.

2. In a pot over medium heat, melt the butter. Add the beer and cream; bring to a simmer.

3. Whisk in the grits and salt. Simmer until the polenta is tender and very thick, whisking occasionally, about 20 minutes.

4. Spoon the polenta onto a parchment-paper-covered baking sheet in circles that are 2" wide and about ½" tall.

5. Bake until the polenta is slightly dry and crisp and has started to brown, 12–15 minutes.

6. Allow to cool; then top with the goat cheese, crumbled bacon, and green onions.

Choose the Right Brew!

The creamy polenta can take a little bit of a hop character but not too much; stay away from the IPAs. Look for a moderately hopped pale ale with lots of malt.

Belgian Ale-CARAMELIZED APPLE AND ONION TARTS

MAKES 14–16 TARTS

1 sheet puff pastry
Egg wash (1 large egg and 1 tablespoon water beaten together)
3 tablespoons unsalted butter
2 tablespoons olive oil
1 large sweet white onion, thinly sliced
2 large Granny Smith apples, peeled, cored, and thinly sliced
2 tablespoons golden brown sugar, packed
½ cup malty dark Belgian ale
2 tablespoons raw honey
1 teaspoon chopped fresh rosemary
1 teaspoon flaky sea salt

Choose the Right Brew!

A fruity, peppery Belgian ale is a great choice for the apples in this recipe.

When it comes to apples, I play favorites. For a raw snack, I'll grab a Fuji, for a salad I'll cut up a Honeycrisp, and for baking I always grab the one my grandma used: the Granny Smith. With a firm flesh that can take a beating without turning to mush and a nice tartness, it's never let me down.

1. Preheat oven to 400°F.

2. On a lightly floured surface, roll out the puff pastry. Using a 3" biscuit cutter or round cookie cutter, cut out 14–16 circles.

3. Line a baking sheet with parchment paper. Place the circles evenly spaced on the baking sheet.

4. Using a fork, poke several holes in each puff pastry circle. Brush the circles with egg wash. Bake for 9–12 minutes or until lightly golden brown. Remove from the oven and press the center of each circle with the back of a spoon to create a flat surface for the onions and apples.

5. In a saucepan over medium heat, melt the butter. Add the olive oil and onions; cook over medium heat, stirring occasionally, until the onions start to soften and turn light brown, about 10 minutes.

6. Add the apples, sugar, beer, and honey. Allow to cook, stirring occasionally, until the apples have softened and started to brown, about 10 additional minutes. Remove from the heat and stir in rosemary.

7. Top each puff pastry circle with apples and onions; sprinkle with sea salt.

BELGIAN ALE RICOTTA TARTS WITH ROASTED FIGS AND HONEY BEER *Caramel Sauce*

MAKES 12–14 TARTS

2 cups whole milk (do not use
    ultrapasteurized)
½ teaspoon salt
¼ cup plus 5 tablespoons Belgian ale,
    divided
2 tablespoons fresh lemon juice
1 pound fresh black mission figs
1 tablespoon olive oil
½ teaspoon salt
½ teaspoon pepper
1 sheet puff pastry
⅓ cup honey
2 tablespoons unsalted butter
1 teaspoon flaky sea salt, such as
    Maldon

When fig seasons hits, it hits hard. Figs go from nonexistent to overabundant. I can't use them fast enough, or have enough creativity to suit the buckets of gorgeous figs that hang from the trees. The first time I roasted figs, I fell in love with what it did to these little beauties. The slightly caramelized char and the soft texture is a great match for some homemade Belgian ale ricotta.

1. In a pot over medium-high heat (do not use an aluminum pan), add the milk, salt, and ¼ cup Belgian ale. Clip a cooking thermometer onto the side of the pan.

2. Bring the liquid to 190°F, stirring occasionally to prevent the bottom from scorching. Keep a close eye on it; the liquid reaches and passes 190°F very quickly and you don't want it rising above 200°F.

3. Remove from the heat, add 2 tablespoons Belgian ale and lemon juice, and stir gently once or twice. It should curdle immediately. Allow to sit undisturbed for about 5 minutes.

4. Line a large strainer with 1 or 2 layers of cheesecloth and place the strainer in the sink over a large bowl. Pour the ricotta into the strainer and allow to drain for 15–30 minutes, then transfer to a bowl. (Ricotta can be made up to 3 days in advance; store in an airtight container in the refrigerator until ready to use.)

5. Preheat oven to 400°F. Cut the figs in half. Add to a baking sheet, drizzle with olive oil, and sprinkle with salt and pepper; toss to coat. Bake for 10 minutes, turn the baking sheet, and bake for an additional 10 minutes.

6. Roll out the puff pastry on a lightly floured surface. Use a 2" biscuit cutter to cut out 24 circles. Add to a baking sheet covered with parchment paper. Prick each circle several times with a fork.

7. Bake for 9–12 minutes or until lightly golden brown. Remove from the oven and press the center of each circle with the back of a spoon to create a flat surface.

8. Add the honey, butter, and remaining 3 tablespoons beer to a pot over medium-high heat. Stir until the butter melts. Bring to a boil; allow to boil for 3 minutes. Remove from the heat.

9. Top each puff pastry circle with ricotta and roasted figs, then drizzle with honey caramel and sprinkle with salt.

Choose the Right Brew!

A bold Belgian triple or quad ale with notes of fruit or cloves will give a nice beautiful balance to the roasted figs that will sit atop the ricotta.

Blackened BEER-BRINED CHICKEN MASA TARTS WITH IPA GUACAMOLE

MAKES 12 TARTS

FOR THE CHICKEN
¾ cup pale ale
2 tablespoons kosher salt
½ cup ice cubes
3 boneless, skinless chicken thighs
1 teaspoon onion powder
1 teaspoon garlic powder
½ teaspoon cumin
½ teaspoon chili powder
½ teaspoon black pepper
½ teaspoon salt
¼ teaspoon smoked paprika
1 tablespoon olive oil

FOR THE MASA TART CRUST
1½ cups masa harina
Pinch salt
1 cup warm pale ale

FOR THE GUACAMOLE
1 large avocado
¼ cup sour cream
1 tablespoon lemon juice
1 tablespoon IPA
¼ teaspoon salt
Pinch cayenne

FOR THE TOPPINGS
1 roasted red bell pepper, sliced
¼ cup crumbled Cotija cheese
2 tablespoons chopped cilantro

I'm going to let you in on a not–so–secret fact about these tarts: They are just small tacos—spicy chicken, guacamole, and a tart crust made out of that same stuff you make corn tortillas from. It's a fancy version of your favorite Tuesday meal.

1. In a pan over medium heat, add the pale ale and salt. Stir just until the salt has dissolved; remove from the heat. Stir in the ice and bring the brine to room temperature.

2. Add the chicken to a bowl or a baking dish and pour the brine over the chicken. Cover and refrigerate for 30 minutes and up to 3 hours.

3. In a small bowl, stir together the onion power, garlic powder, cumin, chili powder, black pepper, salt, and smoked paprika.

4. Remove the chicken from the brine; pat dry with a paper towel. Dredge each piece of chicken in the spice mixture until completely coated.

5. Heat the olive oil in a pan over medium-high heat until hot but not smoking. Add the chicken and cook on both sides until cooked through, about 3 minutes per side. Remove from the pan and slice.

6. In a small bowl, stir together the masa, salt, and warm pale ale, forming a dough that has the consistency of Play-Doh. Form into patties about 2" wide and ½" high.

7. Cook on a griddle or preheated cast-iron skillet until golden brown on each side, about 1 minute per side.

8. In a small bowl, stir together the avocado, sour cream, lemon juice, IPA, salt, and cayenne until well combined.

9. Top each tart with about 1 tablespoon guacamole, a few slices of chicken, a few slices of roasted red peppers, 1 teaspoon Cotija cheese, and a pinch of cilantro.

Choose the Right Brew!

For the chicken and the tart crust, choose a pale ale with a nice amount of malt and moderate to low hops. For the guacamole, look for a citrusy IPA.

Grilled Barbecue CHICKEN AND PEACH MINI PIZZAS

MAKES 8 MINI PIZZAS

FOR THE CRUST
1½ cups flour
1⅛ teaspoons rapid-rise yeast
1 teaspoon sugar
½ cup wheat beer
2 tablespoons oil
½ teaspoon salt

FOR THE CHICKEN
2 boneless, skinless chicken thighs
1 cup wheat beer
½ teaspoon onion powder
½ teaspoon garlic powder
¼ teaspoon smoked paprika
¼ teaspoon chili powder
¼ teaspoon cumin
¼ teaspoon salt
Oil for the grill

FOR THE TOPPING
Barbecue sauce
1 cup shredded mozzarella cheese
1 ripe but firm peach, thinly sliced
¼ teaspoon chopped cilantro
¼ cup chopped red onion

Do you grill pizza? You should. The nice smoky char is exactly what homemade dough needs, and these are just fancy little pizzas. The sweetness of the peaches is a beautiful balance to those grill marks. You may never grill a burger again once you know this is an option.

1. In the bowl of a stand mixer fitted with a dough hook attachment, add the flour, yeast, and sugar. Mix until combined.

2. In a microwave-safe bowl, add the beer. Microwave on high for 20 seconds, test the temperature with a cooking thermometer, and repeat until the temperature reaches 120°F–125°F.

3. Add the beer to the stand mixer and mix on medium speed. Once most of the dough has been moistened, add the oil and salt while the mixer is still running.

4. Turn speed to high and beat until the dough is smooth and elastic, about 8 minutes.

5. Transfer the dough to a lightly oiled bowl; tightly wrap with plastic wrap. Allow to sit in a warm room until doubled in size, 45–60 minutes.

6. Remove from the bowl and add to a lightly floured surface. Knead several times; cut into 8 equal-sized pieces. Form each piece into 4" circles.

7. While the dough is rising, make the chicken. Place the chicken in a bowl and cover with 1 cup beer. Chill 30–60 minutes. Remove from the beer, rinse, and pat dry.

8. Preheat the grill on medium high.

9. In a small bowl, combine the onion powder, garlic powder, smoked paprika, chili powder, cumin, and salt.

10. Sprinkle the chicken on all sides with the spice mixture. Grill the chicken until cooked through, about 5 minutes per side. Remove from the grill and slice.

11. Oil the grill (alternately, you can oil the flatbreads). Grill one side of the flatbread until grill marks appear, about 2 minutes. Flip and very lightly grill the other side, about 30 seconds; then remove from the grill. Place the flatbreads on a flat surface with the well-grilled side facing up. Top with the barbecue sauce, cheese, chicken, sliced peaches, cilantro, and onions. Place back on the grill, close the cover, and cook until the cheese has melted.

Choose the Right Brew!

The mellow breadiness of a wheat beer will work well for both the crust and the chicken brine. Look for one with notes of spice or cloves.

GRILLED BRIE AND PROSCIUTTO FLATBREADS WITH HONEY-ORANGE *Beer Glaze*

MAKES 6 SMALL FLATBREADS

FOR THE FLATBREAD
1½ cups flour
1⅛ teaspoons rapid-rise yeast
1 teaspoon sugar
½ cup summer ale
2 tablespoons oil
½ teaspoon salt

FOR THE TOPPING
½ cup summer ale
3 tablespoons honey
¼ cup freshly squeezed orange juice
    (about ½ navel orange)
8 ounces Brie, sliced
3 ounces prosciutto

A cheese and charcuterie plate is a great party table centerpiece, but putting those same offerings on a little grilled bread and drizzled with a beautiful honey–orange glaze makes it unforgettable.

1. In the bowl of a stand mixer fitted with a dough hook attachment, add the flour, yeast, and sugar. Mix until combined.

2. In a microwave-safe bowl, add the beer. Microwave on high for 20 seconds, test the temperature with a cooking thermometer, and repeat until the temperature reaches 120°F–125°F.

3. Add the beer to the stand mixer and mix on medium speed. Once most of the dough has been moistened, add the oil and salt while the mixer is still running. Turn speed to high and beat until the dough is smooth and elastic, about 8 minutes.

4. Transfer the dough to a lightly oiled bowl; tightly wrap with plastic wrap. Allow to sit in a warm room until doubled in size, 45–60 minutes.

5. Remove from the bowl and add to a lightly floured surface. Knead several times; cut into 6 equal-sized pieces. Form each piece into 4" circles.

6. While the dough is rising, make the glaze. In a large pot (the mixture bubbles up considerably), bring the beer, honey, and orange juice to a boil. Boil, stirring occasionally, until reduced and thickened, about 10 minutes.

7. Preheat the grill on medium high.

8. Place the flatbreads on the grill until grill marks appear, about 3 minutes. Flip and top with Brie. Close the lid and cook until the Brie has

melted and the dough is cooked through, an additional 3 minutes.

9. Remove from the grill and top with prosciutto and glaze.

Choose the Right Brew!

A moderately hopped citrusy summer ale hits the right notes with this.

Hoisin STOUT–BRAISED PORK RIB TARTS

MAKES 24 TARTS

½ cup vinegar
2 teaspoons sugar
3 teaspoons salt, divided
½ cup plus 24 ounces stout, divided
1 cup sliced red onions
2 tablespoons olive oil
½ cup chopped shallots
1 pound country-style pork ribs
1 teaspoon black pepper
½ cup (8 ounces) hoisin sauce
1 sheet puff pastry
¼ cup chopped flat-leaf parsley
2 tablespoons chopped green onions

Choose the Right Brew!

Look for a bold, spicy stout to stand up to the hoisin in this recipe. Look for an imperial stout or an espresso stout.

I discovered the magic of hoisin and pork when I was about twenty-two. It felt like a secret ingredient, this magical sauce that was so sweet, tangy, and deep. Since then I've glazed everything from salmon to tenderloin with this beautiful Chinese sauce.

1. Add the vinegar, sugar, and 2 teaspoons salt to a pot over medium-high heat, stir just until the salt and sugar have dissolved, remove from the heat, and add ½ cup stout.

2. Add the onions to a storage bowl or jar, pour the pickling liquid over the onions, cover, and chill for 30 minutes and up to 3 days.

3. Heat the olive oil over medium-high heat in a large pot or Dutch oven. Add the shallots and cook until softened, about 5 minutes.

4. Sprinkle the pork ribs on all sides with salt and pepper. Add to the pot and sear on all sides. Lower the heat to medium low. Add the hoisin sauce and remaining stout and cook at a low simmer (do not boil) until the ribs are fork tender, about 3 hours.

5. Using two forks, shred while still in the pot. Allow to sit in the liquid for 5–10 minutes.

6. While the pork cooks, make the crusts. Preheat oven to 400°F. Roll out the puff pastry on a lightly floured surface. Use a 2" biscuit cutter to cut out 24 circles. Add to a baking sheet covered with parchment paper. Prick each circle several times with a fork.

7. Bake for 9–12 minutes or until lightly golden brown. Remove from the oven and press the center of each circle with the back of a spoon to create a flat surface.

8. Top each circle with pork, pickled onions, parsley, and green onions.

Beer-Caramelized MUSHROOM GORGONZOLA TART

SERVES 12

2 tablespoons olive oil
2 pounds assorted wild mushrooms
1 medium sweet white onion, sliced
½ teaspoon salt
½ teaspoon black pepper
⅔ cup red ale
1 sheet puff pastry, thawed
2 tablespoons unsalted butter, melted
3 ounces Gorgonzola cheese, crumbled
Coarse kosher or sea salt
2 teaspoons chopped fresh thyme

I spent a few years as a vegetarian. I loved produce and pasta and all other nonmeat-related things, and I decided that mushrooms were my new meat. I'd marinate them, grill them, use them to replace a burger patty, add them to sandwiches. I was set. Although I ended up being seduced back into the world of meat eating by a chili cheeseburger, I've never lost my love of mushrooms.

1. Heat the olive oil in pan over medium-high heat. Add the mushrooms and onion and cook until the mushrooms darken and onions start to soften, about 5 minutes. Add the salt, pepper, and beer; reduce the heat and allow to simmer until the beer is almost completely evaporated.

2. Preheat oven to 400°F. Roll out the puff pastry on a lightly floured surface, then transfer to a baking sheet. Brush the entire pastry with melted butter.

3. Sprinkle the cheese evenly across the tart to within 1" of the edge. Spoon the mushrooms and onions over the cheese. Sprinkle with coarse salt and thyme.

4. Bake until a light golden brown, about 10–12 minutes. Cut into 12 squares.

Choose the Right Brew!

Look for a higher-hop red ale with a bit of light fruitiness to give you a nice flavor with these earthy mushrooms.

Porter-Soaked PLUM, BACON, AND ARUGULA TARTS

MAKES 14–16 TARTS

1 sheet puff pastry
¼ cup melted unsalted butter
1 cup (6 ounces) dried plums
12 ounces porter
3 tablespoons real maple syrup
2 tablespoons balsamic vinegar
½ teaspoon black pepper
6 strips bacon, cooked and chopped
⅓ cup arugula

Choose the Right Brew!

Can you find a maple porter? Maybe one that's a little sweeter than you'd like will work perfect.

Prunes need a rebrand because, let's be honest, they're not very romantic. It's elderly grandmothers and bad images. But the plum! Plums are sexy, beautiful, and mysterious. Plums are invited to the cool parties and drive the fast cars. So in an attempt to save the prune from cultural exile, I will henceforth only refer to them as dried plums, and then they can come to the party.

1. Preheat oven to 400°F.

2. On a lightly floured surface, roll out the puff pastry. Using a 3" biscuit cutter or round cookie cutter, cut out 14–16 circles. Line a baking sheet with parchment paper. Place the circles evenly spaced on the baking sheet.

3. Using a fork, poke several holes in each puff pastry circle.

4. Brush the circles with melted butter. Bake for 9–12 minutes or until lightly golden brown. Remove from the oven and press the center of each circle with the back of a spoon to create a flat surface.

5. In a pot over medium-low heat, add the dried plums, porter, maple syrup, balsamic, and black pepper. Cook for 30 minutes at a very low simmer or until the plums are soft and starting to break down. Add the plums, along with 2 tablespoons cooking liquid, to a food processor; process until smooth.

6. Spread the puff pastry circles with porter-plum jam; top with bacon and arugula.

Chapter 10

SEAFOOD BITES

Drunk Shrimp Diablo . . . 151

Beer and Butter-Poached Scallops with Orange Lime Gremolata . . . 153

Beer-Battered Crab Beignets . . . 155

Beer-Steamed Clams with Linguiça . . . 156

Garlic Chili Beer Butter Shrimp . . . 158

Mango Shrimp IPA Ceviche in Baked Wonton Cups . . . 159

Grilled Prawns with Cilantro Lime White Ale Vinaigrette . . . 161

Miso Stout Salmon Spring Rolls . . . 162

Salmon Meatballs with Asian Porter Sauce . . . 164

Miso Ale–Glazed Shrimp . . . 166

DRUNK SHRIMP *Diablo*

SERVES 6–8

2 tablespoons olive oil
2 tablespoons unsalted butter
1 cup diced white onions
3 cloves garlic, minced
2 tablespoons tomato paste
2 tablespoons garlic chili sauce
1 tablespoon red chili flakes
1 teaspoon chili powder
¼ teaspoon cayenne
⅔ cup IPA
1 pound raw shrimp, deveined (shell removed if desired)
1 cup cherry tomatoes, sliced

The first great beer pairing I ever enjoyed was spicy food and an IPA. The intensity of the hops can stand up really well to a high-heat dish. Make sure to save some of that beer for drinking with this dish to understand what I'm talking about.

1. Heat the olive oil and butter in a skillet over medium heat. Add the onions and sauté until browned, about 3 minutes. Stir in the garlic.

2. Add the tomato paste, chili sauce, red chili flakes, chili powder, cayenne pepper, and beer. Stir over medium heat until well combined.

3. Add the shrimp and tomatoes and cook until the shrimp are pink and have curled. Transfer to a serving dish, or serve right from the skillet.

Choose the Right Brew!

Don't forget that alcohol intensifies heat. The higher ABV (alcohol by volume) the beer is, the spicier the dish will be. Grab a beer with some hops to compete with the spice in this dish.

Beer and BUTTER-POACHED SCALLOPS WITH ORANGE LIME GREMOLATA

12 PIECES

½ cup unsalted butter

12 ounces saison

4 jumbo scallops

2 tablespoons chopped flat-leaf parsley

1 teaspoon orange zest

1 teaspoon lime zest

1 small clove garlic, grated with a Microplane

12 kettle-style potato chips

A few years ago I was at a rooftop party in Los Angeles. The view was amazing, and the food was incredible. I was served tuna tartare on little potato chips and proceeded to follow the waiter around, grabbing bites off his tray every chance I got. The combination of mild fish and crunchy, salty chips just felt perfect. It's a casual and high–impact way to serve up a party appetizer, no rooftop required.

1. In a saucepan over medium heat, melt the butter. Add the beer and scallops; gently simmer (do not boil) until the scallops are opaque on the outside and firm to the touch, about 5 minutes. Remove from the poaching liquid; allow to dry.

2. Slice each scallop into 3 thin disks.

3. In a small bowl, add the parsley, orange zest, lime zest, and garlic; toss to combine.

4. Add 1 scallop disk to each potato chip and top with a pinch of gremolata.

Choose the Right Brew!

A citrusy, peppery saison will give a nice flavor to the mild, white flesh of a scallop.

Beer-Battered CRAB BEIGNETS

MAKES 24 BEIGNETS

¼ cup chopped green onion
6 ounces crab meat
4 ounces cream cheese, softened
½ teaspoon Old Bay Seasoning
1 cup flour
¼ cup cornstarch
1 tablespoon baking powder
Pinch salt
1 cup wheat beer
Canola oil for frying

I was in the South the first time I had a crab beignet. Maybe I'd spent too much time in the health-conscious West, but it was a paper plate full of heaven. I ate far too many and came back the next day for more. It's hard to argue with the South when it comes to deep-fried anything.

1. In a small bowl, gently fold together the onion, crab meat, cream cheese, and Old Bay Seasoning.

2. In a separate bowl, stir together the flour, cornstarch, baking powder, salt, and wheat beer until well combined.

3. In a saucepan over high heat, add about 4" of oil. Using a deep-fry thermometer, bring the oil to 350°F, adjusting the heat to maintain that temperature.

4. Roll about 1 tablespoon of crab mixture into a ball. Using a fork, drop it into the beer batter and roll around until well coated. Drop into the hot oil and fry on all sides until a light golden brown, about 3 minutes. Repeat until all of the crab mixture is used.

Choose the Right Brew!

The breadiness of a wheat beer works well for this.
Grab a beer with some good carbonation.

Beer-Steamed CLAMS WITH LINGUIÇA

SERVES 4–6

1 tablespoon olive oil
1 cup chopped white onions
1 red bell pepper, chopped
½ pound linguiça-style sausage, chopped
12 ounces pilsner
2 pounds littleneck clams
Crusty bread for serving

Tell me this just doesn't look like a bowl full of summer and a good time. Clams are inexpensive and easy to cook, pair well with beer, and require you to dig in with both hands. Grab friends you want to get your hands dirty with and make a big bowl of these little suckers.

1. In a large pot or Dutch oven, heat the olive oil over medium-high heat. Add the onions and peppers and cook until softened, about 5 minutes.

2. Add the linguiça and beer; bring the beer to a low boil. Add the clams and place the lid on the pot. Cook until the clams have opened, about 6 minutes. Discard any clams that haven't opened.

3. Transfer to serving dish; serve with crusty bread.

Choose the Right Brew!

A nice citrusy, moderately hopped pilsner will work well for this.
If you can find something with herbal notes, all the better.

Garlic Chili Beer BUTTER SHRIMP

SERVES 4–6

6 tablespoons unsalted butter
6 cloves garlic, minced
½ cup IPA
1 tablespoon sambal oelek (red chili paste, available in the Asian section of the grocery store)
½ teaspoon smoked paprika
½ teaspoon sweet paprika
¼ teaspoon salt
½ teaspoon black pepper
1 pound raw shrimp, deveined, tail on

You can make this in about 12 minutes. In less time than it takes to answer your e-mail, you can have a big bowl of spicy, beery shrimp. You have no more excuses left.

1. Heat the butter in a pan over medium-high heat until melted. Add the garlic and stir until fragrant, about 30 seconds.
2. Add the beer, red chili paste, smoked paprika, sweet paprika, salt, and pepper; stir until slightly thickened, about 6 minutes.
3. Add the shrimp and simmer (do not boil) until cooked through, about 6 minutes. Skewer with toothpicks, and transfer to a serving platter.

Choose the Right Brew!

Garlic and chili are huge flavors. Get a big beer that can compete. An intense IPA will work well for this dish.

Mango Shrimp IPA CEVICHE IN BAKED WONTON CUPS

MAKES 24 WONTON CUPS

1 pound raw shrimp, peeled and chopped

⅓ cup fresh-squeezed lime juice (about 3 large limes)

⅓ cup fresh-squeezed orange juice (about 1 large Cara Cara orange)

1 large red mango, peeled and diced

1 red bell pepper, diced

12 ounces IPA

½ teaspoon red chili sauce (such as sriracha)

¼ teaspoon sea salt

⅓ cup chopped cilantro

1 large avocado, diced

¼ cup diced red onions

24 wonton wrappers

¼ cup vegetable oil

Ceviche is my go-to when the summer heat is so oppressive I can't even think about turning on my oven. Add in the crunch of a baked wonton cup and you might not want to share.

1. In a small bowl, add the shrimp. Cover with the lime juice and orange juice. Refrigerate until the shrimp have turned pink and "cooked" in the citrus juice, about 2 hours.

2. In a large bowl, add the mango, bell pepper, and IPA. Chill for 30–60 minutes. Drain and return to bowl.

3. Drain the shrimp and add to the mango bowl. Add the chili sauce, sea salt, cilantro, avocado, and onions; toss to combine. Chill until ready to serve.

4. Preheat oven to 350°F. Press the wonton wrappers into the wells of a muffin tin; brush with vegetable oil. Bake until golden brown, 8–12 minutes. Remove from the oven and allow to cool.

5. Fill the cups with ceviche just prior to serving.

Choose the Right Brew!

Try an IPA with tons of fresh hop flavor for this recipe, especially one with strong notes of citrus.

Grilled Prawns WITH CILANTRO LIME WHITE ALE VINAIGRETTE

SERVES 4–6

2 tablespoons lime juice
1 clove garlic
1 teaspoon sugar
1 tablespoon white vinegar
1 teaspoon salt, divided
¼ cup white ale
⅓ cup cilantro
1 teaspoon black pepper, divided
3 tablespoons olive oil
1 pound jumbo shrimp, raw, shell on
3 tablespoons melted unsalted butter

You may drive yourself mad trying to figure out the difference between a prawn and a shrimp, especially since a spot prawn is actually a shrimp and a ridgeback shrimp is actually a prawn. But the good news is that it doesn't matter; they taste the same. Look for large shrimp or prawns, grab a beer, and try not to think too much about it.

1. In a food processor, add the lime juice, garlic, sugar, vinegar, ½ teaspoon salt, beer, cilantro, and ½ teaspoon pepper and process until well combined.
2. While the mixer is running, slowly add the olive oil and process until well combined. Set aside.
3. Preheat grill to medium high.
4. Slice the shrimp in half down the spine, removing the vein and leaving the shells on. Skewer with presoaked wooden skewers, brush with melted butter, and sprinkle with salt and pepper.
5. Grill until cooked through, about 3 minutes per side.
6. Serve with the vinaigrette.

Choose the Right Brew!

A citrusy, herbal white ale will work nicely with the flavors of this recipe.

Miso Stout SALMON SPRING ROLLS

MAKES 8 SPRING ROLLS

3 tablespoons white miso paste
½ cup stout
2 tablespoons brown sugar
2 teaspoons soy sauce
8 ounces salmon
1 cup IPA
½ cup warm water
8 round sheets rice paper
2 tablespoons chopped cilantro
1 cucumber, peeled and sliced into
    matchstick-sized slices
1 tablespoon chopped basil
½ cup bean sprouts

Spring rolls are the perfect summer meal. Light but filling and with a hint of beer, they just feel like a party.

1. In a small bowl, whisk together the miso paste, stout, brown sugar, and soy sauce. Add the salmon, chill, and allow to marinate for 30 minutes.

2. Preheat oven broiler. Remove the salmon and place on a baking sheet covered with aluminum foil. Brush with the marinade. Broil for 3 minutes, remove from the oven, rebrush with the marinade, and broil until just cooked through, about 3 additional minutes. Remove from the oven and allow to cool completely, then flake with a fork.

3. In a pie pan or wide shallow bowl, add the beer and water. One at a time, dip the sheets of rice paper into the liquid (the rice paper will continue to soften as it sits). Remove from the liquid and place on a flat glass or ceramic surface.

4. Add the cilantro, cucumber, basil, bean sprouts, and salmon in a long row down the center of the rice paper circle, fold the edges in over the short sides of the row of ingredients, then roll the spring roll tightly. Chill until ready to serve.

Choose the Right Brew!

An IPA with some citrus or grassy notes will add a
nice balance to the miso and brown sugar.

Salmon Meatballs WITH ASIAN PORTER SAUCE

MAKES 12–14 MEATBALLS

FOR THE MEATBALLS
1 pound salmon, rough chopped, skin removed
1 large egg
1 teaspoon soy sauce
½ teaspoon garlic powder
¼ teaspoon red chili sauce (such as sriracha)
¼ cup panko

FOR THE GLAZE
1 cup porter
2 tablespoons soy sauce
1 tablespoon honey
1 teaspoon sambal oelek (fresh red chili paste)

Until I was an adult, the only meatballs I had were either pork or beef. These meatballs were always rolled in marinara and served over spaghetti. It was what I knew. It wasn't until I was older that I saw the potential that lies in little balls of meat. Salmon, with its rich, fatty meat, is perfect for a strong honey chili sauce, no pasta required.

1. Preheat oven to 350°F. In a small bowl, mix together the salmon, egg, soy sauce, garlic powder, chili sauce, and panko. Form into balls just smaller than golf balls.

2. Place on a baking sheet that has been covered with parchment paper. Bake for 18–20 minutes or until cooked through.

3. In a saucepan over medium-high heat, add the porter, soy sauce, honey, and sambal oelek. Bring to a simmer. Simmer, stirring occasionally, until thickened, about 8 minutes.

4. Gently roll the meatballs in the glaze, skewer with a toothpick, and add to a serving platter.

Choose the Right Brew!

A rich porter with some fruitiness is the right beer for this recipe.

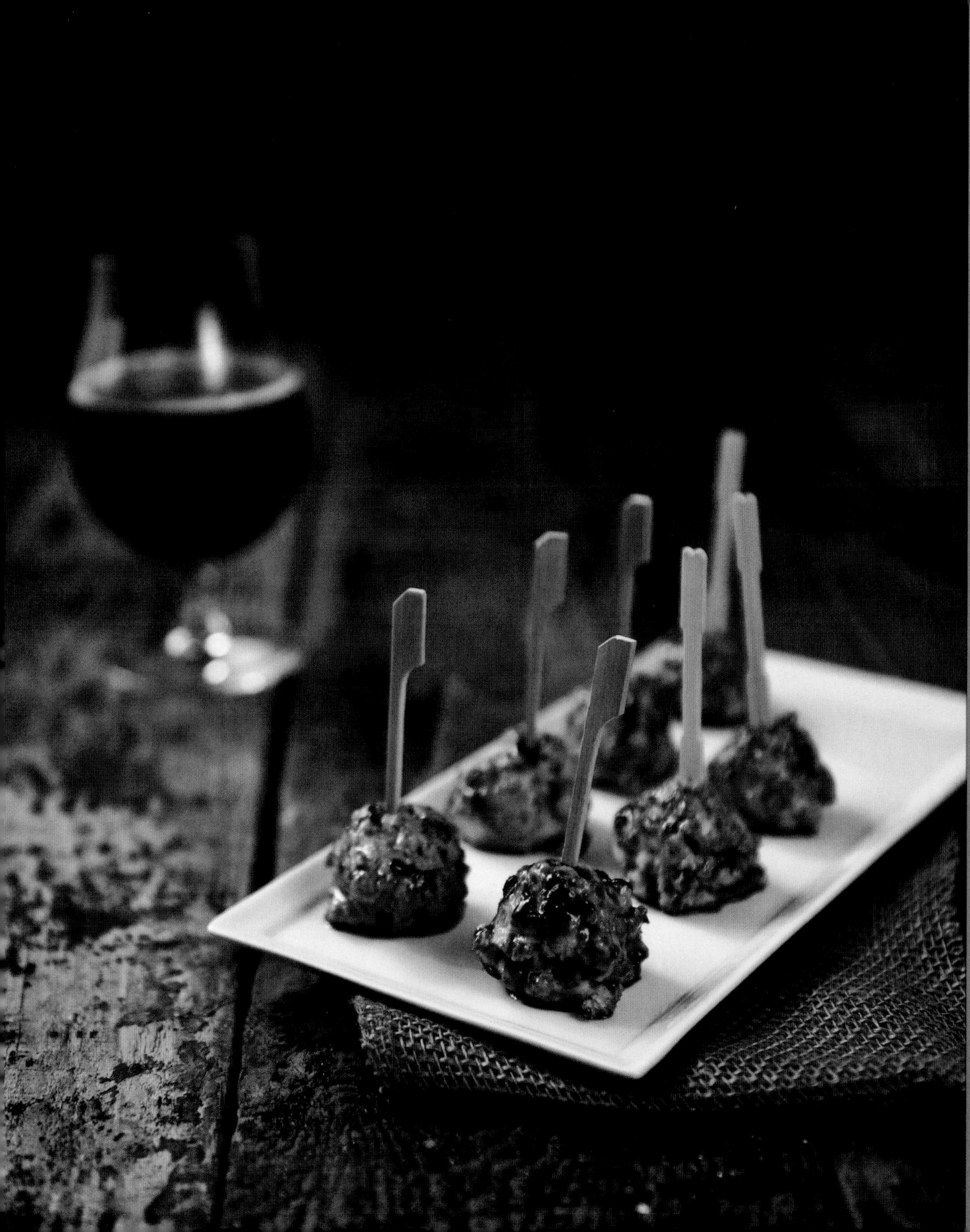

MISO ALE–GLAZED *Shrimp*

⅓ cup pale ale
⅓ cup mirin
¼ cup white miso paste
1 tablespoon white sugar
1 tablespoon brown sugar
1 tablespoon soy sauce
1 teaspoon sesame oil
1 pound raw shrimp, deveined, head and
    shell removed
1 tablespoon olive oil

Miso is such a nice name for fermented bean paste. And shrimp is a better term than sea bug. Although if I named these Fermented Bean Paste Glazed Sea Bugs, you might not want to try them. But in that case, you'd be missing out.

1. In a medium bowl, stir together the pale ale, mirin, white miso paste, white sugar, brown sugar, soy sauce, and sesame oil. Add the shrimp; toss to coat.

2. Cover and refrigerate for 2 hours.

3. Heat the olive oil in a pan over medium-high heat. Remove the shrimp from the marinade and add to the hot pan. Cook on both sides until slightly caramelized and cooked through, about 3 minutes per side. Skewer with toothpicks, and transfer to a serving platter.

Choose the Right Brew!

A pale ale with a good amount of hops and a nice
earthiness is perfect for this shrimp.

Chapter 11
DEEP-FRIED

Beer-Battered Avocado Fries . . . 169

Beer-Battered Mini Corn Dogs . . . 170

Beer-Battered Shrimp with Chipotle Lime Dipping Sauce . . . 171

Beer-Battered Stout Pork Meatballs . . . 172

Beer Churros with Chocolate Stout Sauce . . . 173

Fried IPA Cheddar Mashed Potato Balls . . . 175

Jalapeño Cheddar Beer Hush Puppies . . . 176

Jalapeño Popper Beer Cheese Wontons . . . 177

Raspberry Porter Jelly–Filled Beer Donuts . . . 178

Tempura Beer-Battered Asparagus . . . 181

Beer-Battered AVOCADO FRIES

MAKES 12–15 AVOCADO FRIES

Canola oil for frying
2 cups flour
½ teaspoon salt
½ teaspoon garlic powder
½ teaspoon black pepper
12 ounces wheat beer
3 avocados, ripe but still firm

I first made these when I was throwing a party in Los Angeles. Among the guests were meat-eating, vegan, gluten-free, kosher, and dairy-intolerant people—pretty much as diverse a set of eating preferences as one group can get. In an attempt to please them all I made a taco bar with homemade corn tortillas (which are gluten-free, vegan, and kosher). For the meat eaters I made chipotle braised beef, but for the vegans I didn't want to go the traditional roasted vegetable route. I decided on beer-battered avocados and fresh corn salsa. Most of the avocados were eaten like French fries, and everyone was happy.

1. Fill a large, heavy-bottomed saucepan with canola oil until about 3" deep. Add a deep-fry thermometer and bring the oil to about 350°F, adjusting the heat to maintain that temperature

2. In a large bowl, stir together the flour, salt, garlic powder, and pepper. Add the beer and stir until combined (should have the consistency of pancake batter).

3. Cut the avocados into thick slices (about 4 or 5 per half), making sure to remove the skin and seed.

4. Working in batches, dip the avocado slices into the batter and drop gently into the hot oil; fry until all sides are golden brown, about 3 minutes. Remove from the fryer and allow to drain on a stack of paper towels.

Choose the Right Brew!

Grab a bready wheat beer with lots of carbonation for this recipe.

BEER-BATTERED *Mini Corn Dogs*

MAKES 24 MINI CORN DOGS

Canola or peanut oil for frying
1 cup plus ¼ cup all-purpose flour,
    divided
⅔ cup cornmeal
1 tablespoon brown sugar
1 teaspoon baking powder
1 teaspoon baking soda
1 large egg
¾ cup plus 2 tablespoons pale ale
24 mini hot dogs
24 (4") wooden skewers or toothpicks

These little corn dogs are the perfect casual party appetizer. They are small, portable, battered in beer, and deep–fried. They also remind us all of summer nights and county fairs and the ideal fried food that we begged our parents to let us eat for dinner.

1. Fill a large, heavy-bottomed saucepan with canola oil about 5" deep. Add a deep-fry thermometer and bring the oil to about 350°F, adjusting the heat to maintain that temperature.

2. In a bowl, combine 1 cup flour, cornmeal, sugar, baking powder, and baking soda; stir to combine. Add the egg and the beer and stir until combined.

3. Pour the batter into a tall coffee mug. This will make dipping the corn dogs easier.

4. Skewer all of the mini corn dogs with wooden skewers. Put the remaining ¼ cup flour in a bowl. Roll the hot dogs in the flour, then brush off any excess flour.

5. Holding the skewer, dip the hot dog into the batter until submerged and coated. Slowly place the battered hot dog into the oil. Fry in the oil until dark brown, about 4 minutes.

6. Remove with a slotted spoon and place on a stack of paper towels to drain.

Choose the Right Brew!

A pale ale with a good amount of carbonation will give you a nice lightness to this batter.

Beer-Battered Shrimp WITH CHIPOTLE LIME DIPPING SAUCE

SERVES 4–6

||||||||||||||||||||||||||||||||||||||||||||||||||||||||||||||||||||||||||||||

1 large egg
1 cup all-purpose flour
Pinch cayenne
¼ teaspoon garlic powder
¼ teaspoon salt
1 cup pale ale
Oil for frying
1 pound raw shrimp, deveined, shell and tail removed
1 cup Mexican crema
1 chipotle chili in adobo, minced (plus additional to taste)
1 tablespoon fresh lime juice

When I was a kid, deep-fried shrimp was the pinnacle of culinary perfection. If ever given the choice, a huge plate of battered and fried shrimp was what I'd order, and it'd make me feel like I was eating like a king. To this day, it's such a guilty-pleasure food. I've updated it with the creamy heat of chipotle lime crema and some beer batter, and it's made it even more of a guilty pleasure.

1. Fill a large, heavy-bottomed saucepan with canola oil about 2" deep. Add a deep-fry thermometer and bring the oil to about 350°F, adjusting the heat to maintain that temperature

2. In a bowl, combine the egg, flour, cayenne, garlic powder, and salt; stir to combine. Add the beer and stir until combined.

3. A few at a time, dip the shrimp into the batter, let the excess batter slide off, then add to the oil. Allow the shrimp to cook until golden brown, about 2 minutes on each side. Remove from the pan and add to a stack of paper towels.

4. In a small bowl, stir together the crema, chipotle chili, and lime juice. Add additional chipotle chili to taste, if desired.

5. Serve the shrimp with the dipping sauce on the side.

Choose the Right Brew!

The lightness of a well-carbonated pale ale will do wonders for this beer batter.

Beer-Battered STOUT
PORK MEATBALLS

MAKES 24–28 MEATBALLS

1 pound ground pork
2 tablespoons stout
½ teaspoon salt
½ teaspoon black pepper
¼ cup (1 ounce) shredded Parmesan
1 teaspoon chopped fresh basil
1 cup all-purpose flour
2 tablespoons cornstarch
1 tablespoon baking powder
Pinch salt
1 cup wheat beer
Canola oil for frying

You thought you'd had meatballs before. But you really haven't until you've had them beer battered and deep-fried. The batter locks in those beautiful juices and gives you a flavor-packed mouthful.

1. Preheat oven to 350°F.

2. In a medium bowl, add the pork, stout, salt, pepper, Parmesan, and basil. Stir until just combined.

3. In a separate bowl, stir together the flour, cornstarch, baking powder, and salt. Add the beer and stir until combined.

4. Heat 4" of oil in a pot over medium-high heat and bring to 350°F using a deep-fry thermometer; adjust the heat to maintain that temperature.

5. Roll about 1½ tablespoons meat into a tight ball, then roll in the batter, lifting with a fork to allow excess to drain off. About 3 at a time, drop into the hot oil and cook on all sides until golden brown.

6. Transfer to a wire rack placed over a baking sheet. Bake for 10 minutes or until cooked through.

Choose the Right Brew!

Grab a light, bready wheat beer to add the right texture to this recipe.

Beer Churros WITH CHOCOLATE STOUT SAUCE

SERVES 6

FOR THE CHURROS
½ cup unsalted butter
1 cup wheat beer
¼ teaspoon salt
1 cup all-purpose flour
3 large eggs, beaten
Canola oil for frying
⅓ cup granulated sugar

FOR THE CHOCOLATE STOUT SAUCE
3 ounces dark chocolate
½ cup stout
1 tablespoon cornstarch
2 tablespoons unsalted butter

Choose the Right Brew!

For the churros, look for a nice bready wheat beer. For the chocolate sauce, an imperial stout or a chocolate stout will do nicely.

Years ago I missed my flight out of Madrid for a plate of churros and chocolate sauce. I'd misjudged how long it would take to get to the airport and lingered too long over my favorite bites in all of Spain. Hours later, after booking a return trip home the next day, I went for more churros. An extra night in one of my favorite cities and two plates of churros made me want to miss my flight more often.

1. In a saucepan over medium-high heat, melt the butter. Stir in the beer and the salt. Add the flour, stir until well combined and thickened into a ball, then remove from the heat.
2. Slowly whisk in the beaten eggs until combined.
3. Add the batter to a piping bag with a metal star tip.
4. Heat 4" of oil in a saucepan with a deep-fry thermometer clipped on the side, adjusting heat to maintain 350°F. Gently squeeze 4" ribbons of batter into the hot oil and fry until cooked through and dark golden brown on the outside, about 2 minutes per side.
5. Transfer to a paper towel to briefly drain, then roll in the granulated sugar.
6. To make the sauce, combine all the ingredients in a saucepan over medium-low heat; whisk while cooking until well combined and thickened, about 8 minutes.
7. Serve churros with the Chocolate Stout Sauce on the side.

FRIED IPA *Cheddar Mashed* POTATO BALLS

SERVES 4–6

1½ pounds russet potatoes, peeled and
    chopped
1½ cups shredded Cheddar cheese
½ cup IPA
¼ cup sour cream
1 teaspoon salt
½ teaspoon pepper
1 cup Italian bread crumbs
1 large egg
⅓ cup milk
Canola oil for frying

My favorite Thanksgiving food is mashed potatoes. I always make at least twice as many as can ever be eaten by my guests—there absolutely must be leftovers. Sometimes I like to just eat those leftovers the traditional way, in a nice turkey sandwich. Other times I like to get creative. Deep-fried mashed potato balls are perfect for a post–Black Friday shopping crowd.

1. Cook the potatoes in lightly salted boiling water until fork tender, drain, and return to the pot. Add the cheese, beer, sour cream, salt, and pepper. Using a potato masher, stir and mash until combined. Add to a large bowl, cover, and refrigerate until chilled.

2. In a small bowl, add the bread crumbs. In a separate bowl, beat together the egg and milk.

3. Using a cookie scoop, roll the potato mixture into tight balls, roll in the egg mixture, then in the bread crumbs.

4. Heat 3" of oil in a pot over medium-high heat. Use a deep-fry thermometer to bring the oil to 350°F, adjusting the heat to maintain that temperature.

5. Drop the potato balls into the hot oil and cook until golden brown, about 2 minutes.

Choose the Right Brew!

A citrusy IPA with a bit of malt and some nice carbonation will do well for these potato balls.

Jalapeño CHEDDAR BEER HUSH PUPPIES

MAKES 24 HUSH PUPPIES

1½ cups yellow cornmeal
½ cup flour
2 teaspoons baking powder
1 tablespoon granulated sugar
1 teaspoon black pepper
1 teaspoon salt
¾ cup shredded Cheddar cheese
1 jalapeño, sliced
2 large eggs
¾ cup pale ale
3 tablespoons vegetable oil
Oil for frying (canola or peanut oil)

If I were going to make some laws in this country, requiring hush puppies to be consumed alongside a pint of beer might be one of them. After all, it's illegal to carry an ice cream cone in your back pocket in the state of Alabama, and the legally forced pairing of fried cornmeal and a cold beer makes much more sense.

1. In a large bowl, whisk together the cornmeal, flour, baking powder, sugar, black pepper, and salt. Stir in the cheese and jalapeño.
2. Make a well in the center and add in the eggs, beer, and 3 tablespoons oil; stir until just combined.
3. Heat 4" of oil over medium heat in a saucepan with a deep-fry thermometer clipped to the side, adjusting heat to maintain 350°F.
4. Working in batches of 4 or 5, drop 1 tablespoon dough into the hot oil and fry until golden brown and cooked through, about 3 minutes. Remove from the fryer and allow to dry on paper towels.

Choose the Right Brew!

A pale ale with a good amount of hops and a nice malt backbone is a perfect accompaniment to this recipe.

JALAPEÑO POPPER BEER CHEESE *Wontons*

MAKES 36 WONTONS

8 ounces cream cheese
¾ cup (2 ounces) shredded Cheddar
½ cup IPA
1 tablespoon cornstarch
2 jalapeños, diced
36 wonton wrappers
Oil for frying

Everyone has guilty-pleasure foods. No matter how "foodie" you think you are, there is a food that you love but would never want to be eating if Chef Thomas Keller decided to peek in your kitchen window. For me, that's good ol' American bar food. Nachos, potato skins, jalapeño poppers, onion rings—I love them. Plus, it brings up good memories. Do you have any bad memories of eating fried jalapeños and drinking a beer?

1. In a food processor, add the cream cheese, Cheddar, beer, and cornstarch; process until smooth. Add the jalapeños; pulse to combine.

2. Place a small bowl of water on a flat work surface. One at a time, place a wonton wrapper on the work station and add 1 tablespoon filling to the center. Moisten the edges with water (use either your fingers or a pastry brush), fold the wrapper over, forming a triangle, and press well to seal. Fold two corners in toward the center, using water to secure in place. Repeat for all the wrappers.

3. Add 4" of oil to a saucepan with a deep-fry thermometer clipped to the side; adjust the heat to maintain 350°F.

4. Two at a time, fry the wontons until golden brown, about 1 minute per side. Transfer to a stack of paper towels to drain. Serve warm.

Choose the Right Brew!

A high-ABV IPA with a lot of hops and some citrus is what you want. The alcohol content will kick up the heat a little, and the strong hops will be able to fight through the heat.

Raspberry Porter JELLY–FILLED
BEER DONUTS

MAKES 24 DONUTS

FOR THE DONUTS
2¾ cups bread flour
¾ cup granulated sugar, divided
1 packet rapid-rise yeast (2¼ teaspoons)
¾ cup wheat beer
½ teaspoon vanilla
3 large egg yolks (room temperature)
¼ cup heavy cream (room temperature)
1 teaspoon salt
4 tablespoons unsalted butter, softened
Oil for frying

FOR THE FILLING
½ pound raspberries (fresh or frozen)
1 cup sugar
¼ cup unsalted butter
2 tablespoons cornstarch
Pinch salt
¾ cup porter

First, donuts need to involve two things in order to qualify as real donuts: yeast and a deep fryer. Those baked cake donuts are nothing more than round muffins. Second, there is no such thing as "day old." These suckers need to be eaten right away. Third, the best way to eat a donut is late in the day with a beer, rather than early in the morning with coffee. I hope we can still be friends.

1. In the bowl of a stand mixer fitted with a dough hook, add the flour, ¼ cup sugar, and yeast.

2. Add the beer to a microwave-safe bowl, microwave on high for 20 seconds, test the temperature, and repeat until the beer reaches 120°F–130°F.

3. Add the beer to the stand mixer and mix until most of the flour has been moistened.

4. Add the vanilla; then add the yolks one at a time. Add the cream, salt, and softened butter.

5. Building up speed, beat on high until the dough comes together and gathers around the blade. The dough will be very soft.

6. Add the dough to a lightly oiled bowl, cover, and allow to sit at room temperature for 1 hour or until it doubles in size. Punch down the dough and knead lightly to remove any air bubbles. Place the dough in the fridge and allow to rest for 1 hour.

7. Roll the dough out on a lightly floured surface to 1" thickness. Cut donuts out with a 2" biscuit cutter.

8. Place the donuts on a baking sheet that has been covered with parchment paper. Loosely cover with a towel. Allow to rise at room temperature until doubled in size, about 30 minutes.

9. Fill a large, heavy-bottomed saucepan with oil until about 4" deep. Add a deep-fry thermometer and bring the oil to about 360°F, adjusting the heat to maintain that temperature.

10. Working in batches, fry the donuts on each side until golden brown, about 1–2 minutes per side. Remove from the oil and allow to cool on a wire rack.

11. In a pot over medium-high heat, add the filling ingredients. Simmer, stirring occasionally, until thickened, about 10 minutes. Allow to cool to room temperature.

12. Fill a piping bag with a metal tip with the raspberry filling. Poke a small hole in the side of each donut. One at a time, press the metal tip of the piping bag into the hole, gently squeezing about 2 tablespoons filling into each donut.

13. Add the remaining ½ cup granulated sugar to a small bowl. One at a time, press the donuts gently into the bowl, making sure to coat each side with sugar. Serve immediately.

Choose the Right Brew!

For the dough, grab a bready wheat beer; for the filling, look for a porter with fruity notes.

Tempura BEER-BATTERED ASPARAGUS

SERVES 4

1 cup flour
¼ cup cornstarch
1 tablespoon baking powder
Pinch salt
1 cup wheat beer
Canola oil for frying
1 pound thick asparagus, trimmed

You can pretty much beer batter anything. Vegetables, meat, your car keys. Asparagus is a great choice because even with the high heat you still keep a nice bit of crunch to it. Although not as much crunch as your car keys would give you, but infinitely tastier.

1. In a small bowl, stir together the flour, cornstarch, baking powder, salt, and wheat beer until well combined.
2. In a saucepan over high heat, add about 4" of oil. Using a deep-fry thermometer, bring the oil to 350°F, adjusting the heat to maintain that temperature.
3. A few at a time, dip the asparagus in the batter until well coated, letting the batter drain off for a few seconds before adding to the hot oil.
4. Deep-fry the asparagus until golden brown, 1–2 minutes.
5. Allow to drain and dry on a wire rack; serve immediately.

Choose the Right Brew!

A nicely carbonated wheat beer works perfect for a light beer batter.

Chapter 12

DESSERTS

Belgian Ale Blackberry Sour Cream Ice Cream . . . 185

Barrel-Aged Stout Marshmallows with Stout Chocolate Dipping Sauce . . . 186

Blueberry Beer Mini Pies . . . 188

Chocolate Stout Cupcakes with
Chocolate Stout Cream Cheese Frosting . . . 190

Chocolate Stout Whoopie Pies with Chocolate Cream Cheese Filling . . . 192

Grilled Apricots with Saison Mascarpone and Stout Balsamic Glaze . . . 195

Peanut Butter Stout Mousse–Topped Brownies . . . 196

Miniature Coffee Stout Cinnamon Rolls . . . 198

Miniature Hefeweizen Pound Cakes with Beer Whipped Cream . . . 200

IPA Lemon Bars . . . 202

Belgian Ale BLACKBERRY
SOUR CREAM ICE CREAM

MAKES 1 QUART

1 cup sour cream
1 cup heavy cream
1 cup sugar
1 teaspoon salt
¾ cup Belgian ale
1 tablespoon cornstarch
1 cup fresh blackberries

This is as easy as homemade ice cream gets. No pot on the stove, no eggs to contend with, just everything in a blender before it hits your ice cream maker. Leaves you more time to finish the other half of that beer you opened to make this homemade treat.

1. Put all the ingredients in a blender and blend until smooth.

2. Churn in an ice cream maker according to the manufacturer's specifications until a soft-serve consistency.

3. Pour into an airtight container and freeze until set, about 2 hours.

Choose the Right Brew!

A rich, malty Belgian ale works well with the sweetness
of the cream and tartness of the berries.

Barrel-Aged STOUT MARSHMALLOWS WITH STOUT CHOCOLATE DIPPING SAUCE

MAKES 24–36 MARSHMALLOWS

FOR THE MARSHMALLOWS
Powdered sugar
1 cup barrel-aged stout, flat and cold, divided
3½ envelopes unflavored gelatin (such as Knox)
2 cups granulated sugar
½ cup light corn syrup
2 large egg whites
½ teaspoon salt
3 teaspoons vanilla extract

FOR THE STOUT CHOCOLATE DIPPING SAUCE
10 ounces dark chocolate (50 percent to 60 percent cocoa content)
⅓ cup stout

This is the beginning of next–level s'mores: not just homemade marshmallows, but marshmallows made with a rich, dark stout. It's how campfire stories turn into the stuff of legends.

1. Grease a 9" × 13" baking pan, sprinkle with powdered sugar until well coated, and set aside.

2. In the bowl of a stand mixer, add ½ cup cold, flat beer. Sprinkle with the gelatin. Allow to stand while the sugar is being prepared.

3. In a large saucepan (mixture will bubble up considerably) over medium heat, add the remaining ½ cup beer, sugar, and corn syrup. Stir until the sugar has dissolved.

4. Raise heat to high and allow to boil until the mixture reads 240°F on a candy thermometer (about 6–8 minutes).

5. Once the temperature has been reached, turn off the heat. Turn the mixer on low and slowly pour the hot sugar mixture into the gelatin. Once all the sugar has been added, turn the mixer on high until light and fluffy and tripled in volume, about 6 minutes.

6. While the mixer is running, prepare the egg whites. Add the egg whites to a bowl with the salt. Beat on high with a hand mixer until stiff peaks form.

7. Gently fold the egg whites and vanilla extract into the stand mixer ingredients until just combined.

8. Pour the marshmallow into the prepared baking pan. Sprinkle with powdered sugar. Allow to sit at room temperature until set, about 2 hours. Remove from the pan and cut into squares.

9. To make the chocolate sauce, add the chocolate and stout to a double boiler over medium heat, stir until melted and well combined, then remove from the heat.

10. Serve the marshmallows with chocolate sauce on the side and skewers for dipping. This also works well in a fondue pot.

Choose the Right Brew!

The beer flavor comes through in a big way, so pick a beer with a flavor you really like. A rich barrel-aged beer has a great flavor that is showcased well in these marshmallows.

Blueberry Beer MINI PIES

MAKES 10–12 MINI PIES

|||||||||||||||||||||||||||||||||||||||||||||||||||||||||||||||

3 cups blueberries (fresh or frozen)
¾ cup sugar
3 tablespoons cornstarch
½ teaspoon salt
½ cup blueberry ale
Pastry dough (enough for a single
   standard crust)
1 cup heavy cream
¼ cup powdered sugar
½ teaspoon vanilla extract

It's hard to find a baked good that isn't made just a bit dreamier with the addition of blueberries. Pancakes? Of course. Muffins? The best ones are blueberry studded. And of course, pie. A fresh blueberry pie is hard to beat, especially when you add beer.

1. Preheat oven to 350°F.

2. In a pot over medium-high heat, add the blueberries, sugar, cornstarch, salt, and beer. Boil, stirring occasionally, until thickened, about 8 minutes.

3. Roll the pie dough out on a lightly floured surface. Using a 5" biscuit cutter, cut out 10–12 circles. Line the wells of a muffin tin with the dough circles, pressing into place.

4. Spoon the filling into the muffin tins, about ⅔ full.

5. Bake until the pie crust has turned a dark golden brown, 20–24 minutes.

6. Allow to cool completely before removing from the pan, about 3 hours.

7. In the bowl of a stand mixer, add the cream, powdered sugar, and vanilla; beat on high until medium peaks form. Top pies with whipped cream before serving.

Choose the Right Brew!

Can you find a blueberry beer? They're out there, and will work perfect in these pies. If not, look for a fruity, citrusy pale ale to get the job done.

Chocolate Stout CUPCAKES WITH CHOCOLATE STOUT CREAM CHEESE FROSTING

MAKES 24 CUPCAKES

FOR THE CUPCAKES
4 ounces (about 1 cup) dark chocolate chips
½ cup unsalted butter
¾ cup stout
1¾ cups granulated sugar
2 large eggs plus 1 yolk
3 tablespoons canola oil
⅓ cup buttermilk
1 teaspoon vanilla
1½ cups flour
2 teaspoons baking powder
1 teaspoon espresso powder
½ cup cocoa powder
1 teaspoon kosher salt

FOR THE FROSTING
1 cup (4 ounces) dark chocolate chips
3 tablespoons unsalted butter
½ cup stout
16 ounces cream cheese
4 cups powdered sugar

Julia Child said, "A party without cake is just a meeting." She was a wise, food-loving woman, and I have to agree. You'll need some cake at your party, and these little guys are perfect for a grab-and-go situation rather than a sit-down affair.

1. Preheat oven to 350°F.

2. Make the cupcakes: In the top of a double boiler (or a bowl set over gently simmering water), add the dark chocolate and butter, stirring frequently until just melted. Stir in the stout.

3. In the bowl of a stand mixer, beat the sugar, eggs, and yolk until well combined, light, and fluffy, about 3 minutes.

4. Add the oil, buttermilk, and vanilla; beat until well combined.

5. Slowly add the chocolate, beating until all the ingredients are well incorporated, scraping the bottom to make sure the mixture is well combined.

6. In a separate bowl, whisk together the flour, baking powder, espresso powder, cocoa powder, and kosher salt.

7. Sprinkle the dry ingredients over the wet ingredients; stir until just combined. Line a 24-cup muffin tin with cupcake papers. Fill the cupcake papers ¾ full.

8. Bake for 16–18 minutes. Allow to cool completely.

9. Make the frosting: In the top of a double boiler, add the chocolate and the butter; stir until just melted. Remove from the heat and stir in the stout; allow to cool to room temperature.

(continued)

10. In the bowl of a stand mixer, beat the cream cheese until light and fluffy. Add the powdered sugar and beat until well combined. While the mixer is running, slowly add the chocolate mixture. Mix until well combined.

11. Frost the cupcakes with the chocolate cream cheese frosting.

Choose the Right Brew!

A rich stout with lots of malt and notes of real cocoa is perfect for these cupcakes.

Chocolate Stout WHOOPIE PIES WITH CHOCOLATE CREAM CHEESE FILLING

MAKES 12 WHOOPIE PIES

FOR THE CAKE
2 cups flour
½ cup cocoa powder
½ teaspoon salt
1 teaspoon baking soda
1 teaspoon baking powder
1 cup unsalted butter, softened
½ cup brown sugar
¾ cup white sugar
1 large egg
⅔ cup chocolate stout

FOR THE FILLING
8 ounces cream cheese, softened
½ cup unsalted butter, softened
4 cups powdered sugar
½ cup cocoa powder
2–4 tablespoons chocolate stout

There is a reason we choose to celebrate special occasions with cake. Birthday cakes, wedding cakes, baby shower cakes—it's a big deal to us. If you're throwing yourself a little craft beer party, you need cake in some form. So why not mix it up with these handheld versions? It's still cake; it's just cake for when you have a beer in your other hand and a fork and plate would harsh your vibe.

1. In a medium-sized bowl, stir together the flour, cocoa powder, salt, baking soda, and baking powder; set aside.

2. In the bowl of a stand mixer, add the butter, brown sugar, and white sugar and beat on high until well combined. Add the egg and beat until well combined, scraping the bottom of the bowl to ensure all the ingredients are well combined. Stir in the stout.

3. Add the dry ingredients and stir until just combined, scraping the bottom of the bowl to ensure that all the ingredients are well combined. Refrigerate the dough until chilled, about 30 minutes.

4. Preheat oven to 350°F. Using a cookie scoop, scoop mounds of dough onto 2 greased cookie sheets. Bake until cakes spring back when lightly touched, about 12 minutes. Allow to cool completely.

5. In the bowl of a stand mixer, add the softened cream cheese and butter. Beat on high until well combined and free of any lumps. Add the powdered sugar and cocoa powder; starting on low speed and building up to medium speed, beat until well combined.

6. A tablespoon at a time, add the chocolate stout, allowing to combine completely before adding more until the desired consistency is reached.

7. Spread the filling on the flat side of a whoopie pie; add another (flat side toward the filling) to form a sandwich. Repeat until all the pies are used.

Choose the Right Brew!

Chocolate stout will work well for this recipe, of course, but a rich espresso stout will do just fine as well.

Grilled Apricots WITH SAISON MASCARPONE AND STOUT BALSAMIC GLAZE

SERVES 6–8

¼ cup stout
½ cup balsamic
1 tablespoon honey
Olive oil
2 pounds fresh apricots, cut in half, seeds removed
8 ounces mascarpone, softened
¼ cup powdered sugar
3 tablespoons saison
4 basil leaves, thinly chopped

Grills see a lot of meat—lots of burgers, dogs, and steaks, which is all fine and good. But fruit needs to see those grates just as often. Grilled fruit is a fantastic and easy summertime dessert that just speaks to the spirit of the season.

1. In a pot over medium-high heat, add the stout, balsamic, and honey; bring to a boil. Reduce the heat and allow to simmer until reduced and thickened enough to coat a spoon, about 10 minutes. Set aside.

2. Preheat a grill to medium high. Brush will olive oil. Place the apricots on the grill, cut side down. Grill until the apricots are warmed and grill marks appear, about 2 minutes. Remove from the grill and add to a serving platter.

3. In a small bowl, stir together the mascarpone, powdered sugar, and saison beer. Fill the hole left in the apricots where the seeds were with about 2 tablespoons of the mascarpone mixture.

4. Drizzle with the Stout Balsamic Glaze and sprinkle with basil.

Choose the Right Brew!

For the balsamic glaze, a strong imperial stout will work well; for the mascarpone, look for a saison with herbal or fruit notes.

Peanut Butter STOUT
MOUSSE–TOPPED BROWNIES

MAKES 24 MINI BROWNIES

FOR THE MOUSSE
⅔ cup heavy cream
¼ cup powdered sugar
½ cup creamy peanut butter
3 tablespoons stout

FOR THE BROWNIES
1 cup flour
¼ cup cocoa powder
1 teaspoon baking powder
½ teaspoon salt
1 teaspoon espresso powder
¼ cup granulated sugar
12 ounces (2 cups) dark chocolate chips
6 tablespoons unsalted butter
¾ cup chocolate stout
3 tablespoons vegetable oil
2 large eggs

I can't decide if chocolate and peanut butter are the better pairing or if chocolate and stout take the cake. It doesn't matter; you don't have to choose. Peanut butter, chocolate, and stout all play well together, and the resulting dessert will put all other unions to shame.

1. Preheat oven to 350°F.

2. In the bowl of a stand mixer, add the cream and powdered sugar; beat on high until soft peaks form. Lower speed to medium and slowly add the peanut butter, beating until peaks return. Slowly add the stout; mix until combined. Chill until set, about 30 minutes.

3. In a large bowl, stir together the flour, cocoa powder, baking powder, salt, espresso powder, and sugar; set aside.

4. In the top of a double boiler, add the chocolate chips and butter; stir until melted. Remove from the heat. Stir the stout and vegetable oil into the chocolate.

5. Add the chocolate mixture and the eggs to the dry ingredients and stir until just combined.

6. Pour the batter into mini muffin tins that have been sprayed with cooking spray until ⅔ full.

7. Bake until the tops have set and look dry, about 18–22 minutes. Allow to cool completely.

8. Frost the brownies with the peanut butter mousse prior to serving.

Choose the Right Brew!

Can you find a peanut butter stout? Grab it. If not, look for a smooth milk stout.

MINIATURE *Coffee Stout* CINNAMON ROLLS

MAKES 24 MINI CINNAMON ROLLS
||||||||||||||||||||||||||||||||||||||||||||||||||||

FOR THE DOUGH
3½ cups all-purpose flour
½ cup white sugar
1 packet rapid-rise yeast (2¼ teaspoons)
¼ cup dry milk powder
4 tablespoons unsalted butter
¼ cup cream
¾ cup coffee stout
2 large egg yolks, room temperature
½ teaspoon salt

FOR THE FILLING
½ cup unsalted butter, softened
½ cup white sugar
½ cup brown sugar
2 tablespoons cinnamon

FOR THE FROSTING
8 ounces cream cheese
½ cup unsalted butter
2 cups powdered sugar
¼ cup coffee stout

I can only make cinnamon rolls once a year because I'll eat the entire pan. Most of the time this day is Christmas morning; the house filling with the aroma of cinnamon and dough smells as festive as any pine tree. Although there is some work that goes into these, the end result is well worth the effort. You may even be tempted to make them more than just once a year.

1. In the bowl of a stand mixer fitted with a dough hook, add the flour, sugar, rapid-rise yeast (do not use regular dry active yeast), and dry milk powder. Stir to combine.

2. In a microwave-safe bowl, melt the butter. Add the cream and stout, microwave for 15 seconds, test the temperature, and repeat until the temperature of the liquid reaches 120°F–125°F. Add the liquid to the mixer and stir until incorporated.

3. Add the egg yolks and salt; mix on medium-high speed until the dough comes together and gathers around the blade.

4. Place the dough in a lightly oiled large bowl, cover with plastic wrap, and allow to sit in a warm room until doubled in size, 1½–2 hours.

5. On a lightly floured surface, roll out the dough to an approximately 12" × 16" rectangle.

6. In a bowl, stir together the butter, granulated sugar, brown sugar, and cinnamon. Spread the cinnamon-sugar butter evenly over the dough. Cut the dough in half lengthwise.

7. Starting at the long end, roll each half into a tight log. Cut each log into 1" rolls; place cut side up in a mini muffin tin (or tightly into a baking dish) that has been sprayed with cooking spray. Cover and allow to rise until doubled, about 45 minutes. (To make ahead, the second rise can take place over 12 hours in a refrigerator. Remove from the fridge and

allow to come to room temperature the following day prior to baking.)

8. Heat oven to 350°F. Bake until golden brown, about 22–25 minutes.

9. To make the frosting, beat the softened butter and softened cream cheese until well combined and fluffy. Add the powdered sugar and mix until well combined. Add the beer and mix until light and fluffy. Spread the frosting on the rolls prior to serving.

Choose the Right Brew!

A coffee stout is perfect for this recipe, the richer and bolder the better. The coffee flavor comes through well in the frosting.

Miniature Hefeweizen POUND CAKES WITH BEER WHIPPED CREAM

MAKES 20–24 MINI CAKES

FOR THE CAKE
½ cup unsalted butter
1 cup sugar
¼ cup raw honey
2 large eggs
2 tablespoons canola oil
¼ cup buttermilk
1 teaspoon vanilla extract
1¾ cups all-purpose flour
1½ teaspoons baking powder
½ teaspoon salt
½ cup wheat beer
2 tablespoons fresh lemon juice

FOR THE WHIPPED CREAM
1 cup heavy cream
¼ cup powdered sugar
1 teaspoon vanilla extract
2 tablespoons wheat beer

Fresh fruit or berries (optional)

There is a beautiful simplicity to pound cake. It's moist, dense without being heavy, buttery, and doesn't require frosting. A nice light whipped cream and some fresh berries give this dessert a timeless feel.

1. Preheat oven to 325°F.

2. In the bowl of a stand mixer, beat the butter, sugar, and honey until well combined.

3. While the mixer is running, add the eggs one at a time, scraping the bottom of the bowl between additions.

4. Add the canola oil, buttermilk, and vanilla extract and beat until well combined.

5. In a medium bowl, sift together the flour, baking powder, and salt. In a small bowl, add the beer and lemon juice.

6. Alternating between the dry ingredients and the beer, slowly add both to the mixer, a little at a time, until all the ingredients are just combined.

7. Grease and flour a 9" × 13" baking pan. Pour the batter into the prepared pan. Bake until light golden brown, 20–23 minutes. Remove from the oven and allow to cool completely.

8. Using a 2" circle biscuit cutter, cut out 20–24 circles.

9. In the bowl of a stand mixer, add the heavy cream and powdered sugar. Beat on high until soft peaks form, then slowly add the vanilla and beer, beating until medium peaks form, about 3 minutes.

10. Top the mini cake circles with whipped cream and fruit, if desired.

Choose the Right Brew!

Look for a wheat beer with notes of honey, cloves, or cinnamon.

IPA *Lemon Bars*

MAKES 10–12 LEMON BARS

1 cup flour
⅓ cup powdered sugar
6 tablespoons unsalted butter
¼ teaspoon salt
3 large eggs
1½ cups sugar
¼ cup flour
2 tablespoons cornstarch
⅓ cup freshly squeezed lemon juice
¼ cup IPA
Powdered sugar for dusting

It took me more than a year to finish this recipe. The first few drafts just weren't what I wanted; issues with the crust or the filling prevented me from declaring any of the first few versions as a final product. I finally used powdered sugar in the crust, letting it cool to prevent the crust from blending into the filling, and added a strong IPA to grab the right amount of subtle beer flavor. This version is a keeper.

1. In a food processor, add the flour, powdered sugar, butter, and salt. Process until well combined.

2. Press into the bottom of a greased 8" × 8" pan (for a 9" × 13" pan, double the entire recipe). Chill for 15 minutes.

3. Preheat oven to 350°F.

4. Bake for 20–25 minutes or until golden brown. Remove from the oven and allow to cool to room temperature, about 15 minutes (this will help the crust and the filling to stay in two distinct layers).

5. In a large bowl, whisk together the eggs, sugar, flour, and cornstarch. Add in the lemon juice and beer; stir until combined. Pour the filling over the cooled crust. Bake until the center has set, about 20–25 minutes. Allow to cool slightly before refrigerating. Chill for 2–3 hours before cutting. Dust with powdered sugar before serving.

Choose the Right Brew!

A citrusy, bold IPA is the best choice for this. Look for something with a fresh hop profile and lots of citrus.

U.S./METRIC CONVERSION CHART

VOLUME CONVERSIONS

U.S. Volume Measure	Metric Equivalent
⅛ teaspoon	0.5 milliliter
¼ teaspoon	1 milliliter
½ teaspoon	2 milliliters
1 teaspoon	5 milliliters
½ tablespoon	7 milliliters
1 tablespoon (3 teaspoons)	15 milliliters
2 tablespoons (1 fluid ounce)	30 milliliters
¼ cup (4 tablespoons)	60 milliliters
⅓ cup	90 milliliters
½ cup (4 fluid ounces)	125 milliliters
⅔ cup	160 milliliters
¾ cup (6 fluid ounces)	180 milliliters
1 cup (16 tablespoons)	250 milliliters
1 pint (2 cups)	500 milliliters
1 quart (4 cups)	1 liter (about)

WEIGHT CONVERSIONS

U.S. Weight Measure	Metric Equivalent
½ ounce	15 grams
1 ounce	30 grams
2 ounces	60 grams
3 ounces	85 grams
¼ pound (4 ounces)	115 grams
½ pound (8 ounces)	225 grams
¾ pound (12 ounces)	340 grams
1 pound (16 ounces)	454 grams

OVEN TEMPERATURE CONVERSIONS

Degrees Fahrenheit	Degrees Celsius
200 degrees F	95 degrees C
250 degrees F	120 degrees C
275 degrees F	135 degrees C
300 degrees F	150 degrees C
325 degrees F	160 degrees C
350 degrees F	180 degrees C
375 degrees F	190 degrees C
400 degrees F	205 degrees C
425 degrees F	220 degrees C
450 degrees F	230 degrees C

BAKING PAN SIZES

American	Metric
8 × 1½ inch round baking pan	20 × 4 cm cake tin
9 × 1½ inch round baking pan	23 × 3.5 cm cake tin
11 × 7 × 1½ inch baking pan	28 × 18 x 4 cm baking tin
13 × 9 × 2 inch baking pan	30 × 20 × 5 cm baking tin
2 quart rectangular baking dish	30 × 20 × 3 cm baking tin
15 × 10 × 2 inch baking pan	30 × 25 × 2 cm baking tin (Swiss roll tin)
9 inch pie plate	22 × 4 or 23 × 4 cm pie plate
7 or 8 inch springform pan	18 or 20 cm springform or loose bottom cake tin
9 × 5 × 3 inch loaf pan	23 × 13 × 7 cm or 2 lb narrow loaf or pate tin
1½ quart casserole	1.5 liter casserole
2 quart casserole	2 liter casserole

GLOSSARY of BEER TERMS

abbey, abbaye, abdj bier. For many years this meant a beer was made in an abbey or by monks. However, today it means that the beer is made in the Trappist tradition.

Adam's ale. Water; another way of calling a beer watery or weak.

additives. Preservatives that some brewers sometimes add in order to lengthen shelf life or enzymes that produce an artificial head, to give their beer the appearance of having body. Mostly found in beers manufactured by larger brewers.

adjuncts. Adjuncts are added to the barley malt during brewing. This is done to create certain effects. Crafters use wheat and oats to gain special flavors. Many larger manufacturers add corn as a cheap substitute, or as a way to make their barley go a little further.

alcohol. Alcohol results in beer as part of the traditional brewing methods through the fermentation of grains. A beer does not have to contain alcohol to be called beer. Most beers contain 4 to 5 percent alcohol.

ale. A beer made with top-fermenting yeast, usually characterized by a fruitiness of flavor. Ales do not take much time to create from brewing to serving. A lager, for example, needs to be stored before serving, while an ale does not. According to some state laws, ale denotes a higher alcoholic content than a lager. The world brewing community does not see it this way. Ales range from bitter to sweet and vary greatly in their alcoholic content.

aleberry (alebrew, albrey, alebery). A spiced ale, dating from the Renaissance, that was brewed with sugar, spice, and bits of bread.

ale-conner. In England, an inspector of ale. Shakespeare's father was an ale-conner.

alecy. A description of madness thought to be induced by beer.

alegar. Malt vinegar.

all barley. A beer brewed from only barley malt, with no other adjuncts, additives, grains, corn, rice, or sugars.

all malt. A beer brewed from only malted grains, with no other adjuncts, additives, corn, rice, or sugars.

alt. "Old" in German, as in *altbier*, meaning "old beer."

altbier. "Old beer" in German; this is the type of brewing that preceded lagers.

barley. The central ingredient to brewing beer. By placing mature barley in a kiln and firing it, malt is created, which helps give beer its flavor and color.

barley wine. Not really a wine at all, but a very strong ale with alcohol usually twice that of strong beers. Barley wine is brewed in colorations ranging from pale to dark. The term is English, coming from the fact that its alcohol content was closer to that of wine.

barrel. One barrel equals 31 U.S. gallons of beer. Usually used to measure a brewery's output.

bayerisch. German for "Bavarian."

beer. Any drink made from fermented grains and, more than likely, hops. *Beer* is the generic term for an entire family of beverages. Ales, lagers, porters, and stouts are all considered beer. In America, beer is usually meant to be lager, while the English tend to mean ale when they ask for a beer.

Belgian lace. The residue left on the inside of a glass after the head expires. Belgium has been famous for centuries for both its beers and its lace.

Berliner weisse. Also known as wheat beer. Known for its low alcoholic content, this is a milky, white-ish beer that is highly carbonated.

bier. German for "beer."

bière ordinaire. French for "house beer."

bière de garde. A strong ale from France. Meant to be laid down or cellared.

bierwurst. A German sausage flavored heavily with garlic. Usually dark.

bitter. An English ale brewed with high hop content. Designated as Special, Best, and Extra Special in order of alcohol content, with Special the lowest and Extra Special the highest, between 5 and 6 percent alcohol.

black and tan. A mixture of stout or porter with golden ale or lager.

bock. German for "billy goat," refers to a strong beer. A lager. In Germany a bock may be of many colors; however, outside Germany it usually means a dark beer.

Bock beer averages well above 6.25 percent alcohol by volume. It is usually served seasonally, once a year, depending on what country you are in. There are many kinds of bocks, including maibock, doppelbock, and weizenbock.

bottle-conditioned. Usually an ale. Yeast is added to the beer right before bottling to further the fermentation process and increase carbonation. This usually refers to a craft beer that is unpasteurized. Known in the winemaking industry as *méthode champenoise*.

bottom-fermented. How lager is brewed. Made with lager yeasts, the beer ferments at the bottom of the tun, resulting in a clearer brew than a top-fermented beer.

brewery. A place where beer is made in large quantity for sale, either retail or wholesale. The difference between a microbrewery and a brewery is that breweries produce more than 25,000 barrels of beer in any given year.

breweriana. Of or referring to beer memorabilia.

brewpub. A tavern, bar, or pub that brews its own beers. The beer is usually available on tap and, in some cases, is bottled for retail sale. Some people refer to these as microbreweries. The difference between a brewpub and a microbrewery is that a microbrewery sells larger amounts of beer and sells its beer to beer retailers.

brewer's inch. The last inch of beer in a pot or vat; the lees.

brown ale. A dark, sweet ale, usually brewed in the south of England (sweet), in the northeast of England (less sweet, reddish), and in Flanders (brown, sour). Relatively low in alcohol.

burdock. An herb once used before hops for flavoring.

buttered ale. Ale with sugar, butter, and cinnamon.

cask-conditioned. A draft beer usually brewed in the cellar of a pub. An unpasteurized beer that goes through a secondary fermentation in the cask in which it is sold.

cauliflower. The result of the brewing of ale; the top layer of yeast.

collar. Another name for the head on the beer.

contract brew. A beer brewed for a distributor by a brewery not owned by the distributor. Usually the distributor supplies the recipe. Bottling does not necessarily take place at the brewery. Some well-known small beers are made in this fashion.

coppery. The vessels, vats, or pots that beer is brewed in; usually made of stainless steel.

cream ale. An American ale brewed with both the bottom- and top-fermentation process at the same time. This produces a light pale ale, golden in color.

dark beer. A generic term. Usually refers to a dark lager.

decoction. Style of lager determined by the way in which the malt is mashed.

deglaze. To remove the remaining bits of sautéed meat or vegetables from a pan by adding a liquid (such as beer) and heating. Used to create the base for a sauce.

diät pils. A beer originally brewed for diabetics. By very careful fermentation, carbohydrates are eliminated, usually resulting in a very strong beer. Germany has laws now that require many brewers of this beer to reduce the alcohol content before finishing.

doppelbock. German for "double bock." Usually very dark and sweet. An extra-strong version of bock.

Dort. Short for Dortmunder, especially in the Netherlands and Belgium.

Dortmunder. A beer brewed in Dortmund, usually of the export style.

draft beer in a can. In an attempt to create the creaminess, richness, and foaminess of draft beer, nitrogen is added to the can during canning.

dry beer. Japanese name for diät pils, milder than the German original, and made even more mild in America. A dry beer in America has little taste and finish.

dry hopping. When fresh hops are added to a cask of beer.

dunkel. German for "dark." Dark beers are sometimes referred to as dunkels.

eisbock. When a doppelbock beer is frozen and the ice is removed, the taste and alcohol level of the beverage left over is intensified.

export. A lager that usually has more body than a pilsner. The term in Germany refers to a lager that has less hops than most common pilsners. The beer is drier than a pilsner as well. Often classified as premium, which means little.

faro. A lambic beer that is sweetened by the addition of candy sugar.

fermentation. The chemical reaction whereby yeast organisms turn sugars into alcohol and carbon dioxide.

festbier. Beer made for a festival. Refers to any beer. Most of these beers are high in alcoholic content.

framboise (frambozen). A lambic made with raspberries.

fruit beer. Any lager or ale that has had fruit added to it during any stage of brewing.

genuine draft. A sterile, filtered, unpasteurized bottled or canned beer.

gravity. A weighing system used to judge the heaviness of a beer. When a beer is said to have gravity, this means that it has body and heft. In actuality, it judges the amount of hops in a beer.

grist. Barley that has been malted and milled. It is thrown in the mash tun and heated with hot water to produce the wort.

gueuze. A lambic beer that is a mixture, not necessarily in equal parts, of old and young lambic beer.

haute fermentation. French for "top fermentation."

heavy. Term used in northern England to speak of the richness and gravity of a beer.

hefe. German for "yeast." Often identifies the beer as either sedimented or that which has had yeast added to it just before bottling. See *bottle-conditioned.*

hell (or helles). German for "pale." Generally a golden color.

hops (*Humulus lupulus*). The female hops plant is used in full flower to add different flavors, bitterness, and aroma to beer. In earlier times it was thought to be a preservative.

ice beer. An attempt to emulate and market an Eisbock-like beer, beer is frozen either during the fermentation process or sometime after maturation during the storage period. The water is largely removed, and then the beer is reconstituted later.

imperial stout. A stout brewed in England for the czars and sent to Saint Petersburg. The alcoholic content was reportedly somewhere between 7 and 10 percent.

India pale ale. Originally a bitter beer brewed in Britain and exported to soldiers in India. It was made strong so that the beer would stand the long voyage and still be flavorful when opened halfway around the world. Today the moniker generally indicates a premium pale ale.

infusion. An English style of mashing.

kellerbier. A lager of low carbonation, very high in hops. An unfiltered beer.

kettle. Another name for the coppery, or vats, where beer is brewed.

klosterbier. German for "cloister beer." Implies that the beer was or is brewed in a convent or monastery.

Kölsch. A light ale from Cologne, Germany.

krausen. This is the German term for bottle-conditioning, where yeast is added just before bottling so that a higher carbonation develops in the bottle.

kriek. A lambic beer made with cherries.

kruidenbier. Dutch for "spiced beer."

kvass. A beverage very much like beer, made in Russia with rye bread.

lager. From the German word "storehouse." Lagers are made with a bottom- or cold-fermentation and aged for a period of up to several months to complete the fermentation. Because of their longer fermentation process, lagers are generally smoother, crisper, and more subtle in taste than ales. Lagers are always served cold. While British lager tends to be golden in color, European lagers tend to be darker. In Germany and some Dutch-speaking countries it is the term for the house beer.

lambic beer. A wheat beer, most notably from Belgium, that is fermented with wild yeasts. Finishes almost like a cider.

lamb's wool. A concoction of ales, spices, and apples.

light ale. Not to be confused with the American version of light beer, this has nothing to do with calories. In England it is the opposite of a bitter beer, usually dark. Sometimes refers to an ale with less alcoholic content, but not necessarily.

light beer. A low-calorie, low-alcohol beer. A watery version of pilsner with little flavor or body. Usually between 3 and 4 percent alcohol by content.

maibock. A lager made in the spring to celebrate the new season; usually light in color.

malt. The basic ingredient in almost every beer. Barley that has been soaked and begins to sprout. It is then fired in a kiln and ground down. This firing process determines the color and flavor of beer.

malt liquor. Often associated with cheap beers, these tend to be American ales that range up to 7.5 percent alcohol by content. More often than not they are sweet.

Märzen (or Märzenbier). German for "March." A lager made in March for the Oktoberfest of the coming year. Usually a beer rich in malt flavors. Often amber-red in color.

mash tun. A large copper or stainless steel pot or vat.

microbrewery. A small brewery, sometimes referred to as a craft brewery. A microbrewery generally produces between 15,000 and 35,000 barrels of beer a year. Many small brewers have far exceeded that number but continue to be known as microbrewers.

mild. A beer light in hops. These are usually dark and not very high in alcoholic content.

Müenchener/Münchner. A beer-brewing style that is largely associated with Munich. These are dark lagers that are often spicy and generally not high in alcohol.

obergärig. German for "top-fermented."

Oktoberfest. A festival in Germany that takes place in the fall; millions come every year from all over the world to take part in the festivities. It is a celebration of German history and culture—and, of course, beer. In ancient Germany the Märzenbier (the March beer) was made in March and was drunk in October to celebrate the harvests. The modern Oktoberfest lasts sixteen days, beginning in late September and ending in October. Oktoberfest found its roots in 1810 in an effort by Germans to celebrate the marriage of the crown prince of Bavaria. Smaller festivals around the world also coincide with this internationally renowned festival.

old. An English appellation given to dark beers. These beers tend to be dark and strong. They are not old in recipe or age.

oscura. Spanish for "dark" beer.

pale ale. A beer lighter in color. Generally not as bitter as India pale ale. Usually ranging from golden to reddish.

pilsener/pilsner/pils. A lager or bottom-fermented beer, usually light in color. It draws its name from the town of Pilsen, in Bohemia in the Czech Republic.

The original brewer of this beer was Josef Groll, and the beer, first brewed and sold in 1842, is known as Pilsner Urquell. It is a dry beer and has a wonderful hoppiness about it. The Americanized pilsner is lighter in color, flavor, and hops.

porter. Almost black, porter is a bitter, dark lager. First brewed in England around the 1730s, it got its name from the carters and porters who tended to substitute it for a meal. Porter was largely forgotten until recently. Many American microbreweries were responsible for reviving this beer.

rauchbier. A lager largely brewed in Franconia and Hamburg. The style is achieved by using smoked malts. Other variations include smoking the malt with peat moss (Scottish style) or throwing fire-heated rocks into the malt.

Reinheitsgebot. German laws that govern brewing in that country. Originally known as the Bavarian Purity Law of 1516 and now called the German Beer Purity Law. The law states that beer can only be brewed from water, hops, barley, malt, and yeast.

saison. A Belgian summer ale that is sometimes bottle-conditioned.

schwarzbier. A beer made famous in Bad Köstritz, Germany. A very, very dark beer.

Scotch ale. A very dark, strong ale. Many are brewed in Scotland, hence its name. Some microbreweries have begun brewing this style of beer.

shandy. A drink made of half beer and half lemonade.

steam beer. A product of the California Gold Rush, steam beer was America's first real addition to the craft of brewing. Using large shallow vats called clarifiers, lager yeast is used at high temperatures, as if one were brewing an ale. This produces a beer with the complexities of both an ale and a lager.

stout. A very dark, high-hop content ale. The most famous brewer of stout and the originator of this style is Guinness of Ireland. Stouts vary from dry to sweet, but all have sugar added to them at one stage or another. Guinness tends to be on the dry side and comes in a variety of alcoholic strengths.

top-fermented. The fermentation process used to make ale.

Trappist. A bottle-conditioned, sugar-added lager made by monks in only six breweries in the world (five in Belgium, one in Holland). While others might attempt a Trappist-style beer, only these monasteries are allowed to market their beers with this term on the label. Unusually high in alcoholic content, sometimes reaching 12 percent or more, they are fruity and some of the most highly prized beers in the world.

tripel. Dutch, meaning a brewer's strongest beer. Can be a lager, but most often is an ale.

trub. German for "sediment."

Ur-/Urquell. German for "original source." A term that means the first or original brewer; i.e., Pilsner Urqell is the original source or brewer of pilsner: the original pilsner.

Vienna. A reddish beer once made famous in Vienna, Austria. Also known as Vienna malt.

weisse/weissbier/weizenbier. Wheat beer. Often served with lemon, this is an ale of extremely light color, mostly served during the summer. The beer is brewed with mainly wheat malt.

white. Another term for a wheat beer.

wiesen/wies'n. German for "meadow." This is a beer especially brewed for an occasion or a festival, like Oktoberfest.

witbier. Dutch for "white beer." Another name for white, wheat, or weisse beer.

wort. The stage in the brewing process before the addition of the yeast. The juices that result from the cooked barley.

yeast. A fungus or microorganism that causes fermentation, turning sugar into alcohol and carbon dioxide. Lager yeast is known as *Saccharomyces pastorianus*, and ale yeast is known as *Saccharomcesy cerevisiae*.

zwickelbier. An unfiltered beer in Germany, usually characterless.

zymurgy. The science of brewing and fermentation, a branch of chemistry.

INDEX

Note: Page numbers in **bold** indicate recipe category lists.

Alcohol
intensifying heat, 16, 19, 21
    tenderizing meat, 15
Apples
    Belgian Ale–Caramelized Apple and Onion Tarts, 131–33
    Brown Ale Pork and Apple–Filled Buns, 100–101
Apricots, grilled with saison mascarpone and stout balsamic glaze, 194–95
Artichokes
    Seven-Layer Jalapeño IPA Hummus Dip, 88
    Spinach Artichoke Beer Cheese Crostini, 75
Asian Porter Sauce, 164
Asparagus, tempura beer-battered, 180–81
Avocados
    Beer-Battered Avocado Fries, 169
    Horseradish Guacamole, 37
    IPA Guacamole, 138–39
    Peach Salsa and Beer-Battered Avocado Crostini, 72
    Porter Harissa Crostini, 69–70

Baba ghanoush, roasted garlic and smoked porter, 90–91
Bacon
    Beer and Bacon Dip, 79
    Goat Cheese and Bacon Tarts with Pale Ale Polenta Crust, 130
    Maple Porter–Glazed Bacon-Wrapped Dates, 50–51
    Porter-Soaked Plum, Bacon, and Arugula Tarts, 147–48
Balsamic glaze, stout, 195
Banh mi sliders, pork stout meatball, 36
Basil, in Beer Pesto, 96–97
Beans
    Beer-Braised Carnitas Crostini, 61–62

Chipotle Porter Hummus, 81–82
Parsley White Bean Beer Cheese Dip, 86
Porter Black Bean Dip, 87
Seven-Layer Jalapeño IPA Hummus Dip, 88
Beef
    about: beer/alcohol tenderizing, 15
    Beer-Battered Mini Corn Dogs, 170
    Grilled Beer-Marinated Prosciutto-Wrapped Beef Tenderloin Skewers, 44
    Grilled Rosemary Porter Fillet Tip Skewers, 45–46
    Stout French Dip Sliders, 39
    Stout-Marinated Beef Satay with Beer Peanut Sauce, 56–57
Beer. See Craft beer; *specific beer types*
Beer and Bacon Dip, 79
Beer and Butter–Poached Scallops with Orange Lime Gremolata, 152–53
Beer and Sriracha–Candied Nuts, 113–14
Beer-Battered Avocado Fries, 169
Beer-Battered Crab Beignets, 154–55
Beer-Battered Gorgonzola-Stuffed Olives, 115
Beer-Battered Mini Corn Dogs, 170
Beer-Battered Shrimp with Chipotle Lime Dipping Sauce, 171
Beer-Battered Stout Pork Meatballs, 172
Beer-Braised Asian Pork Sliders with Fried Wonton Buns, 29–30
Beer-Braised Carnitas Crostini, 61–62
Beer-Brined Chicken and Strawberry Salsa Lettuce Wraps, 95
Beer-Candied Pecans, 116
Beer-Caramelized Mushroom and Spinach Hand Pies, 98
Beer–Caramelized Mushroom Gorgonzola Tart, 146
Beer Churros with Chocolate Stout Sauce, 173–74
Beer Peanut Sauce, 56
Beer Pesto and Beer Ricotta Mini Calzones, 96–97
Beer-Pickled Peaches, 68

Beer-Poached Lobster Sliders, 31

Beer Sausage Stuffed–Crispy Fried Olives, 117

Beer-Soaked Cantaloupe and Mozzarella Skewers, 43

Beer-Steamed Clams with Linguiça, 156–57

Beer terms, glossary of, 205–12

Beignets, beer-battered crab, 154–55

Belgian ale

    Beer-Braised Lamb Shank Tarts with Belgian Cherry Sauce, 127–29

    Beer-Caramelized Mushroom and Spinach Hand Pies, 98

    Belgian Ale Blackberry Sour Cream Ice Cream, 185

    Belgian Ale–Caramelized Apple and Onion Tarts, 131–33

    Belgian Ale–Marinated Grilled Steak Crostini with IPA Chimichurri, 63–64

    Belgian Ale Ricotta Tarts with Roasted Figs and Honey Beer Caramel Sauce, 134–37

    Curried Belgian Ale Mixed Nuts, 121

    Tomato Beer Jam–Filled Biscuits, 109–10

Belgian Cherry Sauce, 127–29

Berries

    Belgian Ale Blackberry Sour Cream Ice Cream, 185

    Blackberry Stout Wontons, 99

    Blueberry Beer Mini Pies, 188–89

    Raspberry Porter Jelly–Filled Beer Doughnuts, 178–79

    Strawberry Salsa, 95

Biscuits. *See* Breads and buns

Blackberries

    Belgian Ale Blackberry Sour Cream Ice Cream, 185

    Blackberry Stout Wontons, 99

Blueberry ale, in Blueberry Beer Mini Pies, 188–89

Book overview, 11

Breads and buns. *See also* Hand pies, wraps, and rolls

    Brown Ale Pork and Apple–Filled Buns, 100–101

    Fried Wonton Buns, 29–30

    Miniature Coffee Stout Cinnamon Rolls, 198–99

    Pepper Beer Biscuits, 32–33

    Raspberry Porter Jelly–Filled Beer Doughnuts, 178–79

    Tomato Beer Jam–Filled Biscuits, 109–10

Brown ale

    Beer-Brined Chicken and Strawberry Salsa Lettuce Wraps, 95

    Brown Ale Pork and Apple–Filled Buns, 100–101

    Crispy Shallots and Parmesan Beer Cheese Dip, 83

Brownies, peanut butter stout mousse–topped, 196–97

Buffalo Chicken Beer Cheese Dip, 80

Buns. *See* Breads and buns

Calzones, mini, 96–97

Cantaloupe, in Beer-Soaked Cantaloupe and Mozzarella Skewers, 43

Caramel sauce, honey beer, 134–35

Carnitas crostini, beer-braised, 61–62

Cheese

    Beer and Bacon Dip, 79

    Beer-Battered Gorgonzola-Stuffed Olives, 115

    Beer-Braised Carnitas Crostini, 61–62

    Beer-Caramelized Mushroom Gorgonzola Tart, 146

    Beer Ricotta, 96–97

    Beer-Soaked Cantaloupe and Mozzarella Skewers, 43

    Belgian Ale Ricotta Tarts with Roasted Figs and Honey Beer Caramel Sauce, 134–37

    Buffalo Chicken Beer Cheese Dip, 80

    Chocolate Cream Cheese Filling, 192–93

    Chocolate Stout Cream Cheese Frosting, 190–91

    Crispy Shallots and Parmesan Beer Cheese Dip, 83

    Fried IPA Cheddar Mashed Potato Balls, 175

    Goat Cheese and Bacon Tarts with Pale Ale Polenta Crust, 130

    Goat Cheese Crostini with Beer-Pickled Peaches, 68

    Grilled Apricots with Saison Mascarpone and Stout Balsamic Glaze, 194–95

    Grilled Brie and Prosciutto Flatbreads with Honey-Orange Beer Glaze, 142–43

    IPA-Soaked Watermelon Skewers with Cotija and Mint, 48–49

    Jalapeño Cheddar Beer Hush Puppies, 176

    Jalapeño Popper Beer Cheese Wontons, 177

    Maple Porter–Glazed Bacon-Wrapped Dates, 50–51

    Parmesan Crab Beer Cheese Crostini, 71

    Parsley White Bean Beer Cheese Dip, 86

    Seven-Layer Jalapeño IPA Hummus Dip, 88

    Smoked Salmon and Pale Ale Chive Cream Cheese Crostini, 73–74

    Spinach Artichoke Beer Cheese Crostini, 75

    Stout-Soaked Mushroom and Herbed Goat Cheese Crostini, 76

    Triple-Chili Beer Cheese Dip, 89

    wraps with. *See* Hand pies, wraps, and rolls

Cherries, in Belgian Cherry Sauce, 127–29

Chilies. *See* Pepper(s)

Chili Lime Beer Roasted Peanuts, 118

Chipotle Lime Dipping Sauce, 171

Chipotle Porter Hummus, 81–82

Chocolate

Barrel-Aged Stout Marshmallows with Stout Chocolate
    Dipping Sauce, 186–87
Beer Churros with Chocolate Stout Sauce, 173–74
Chocolate and Stout–Coated Almonds, 119
Chocolate Cream Cheese Filling, 192–93
Chocolate Stout Cupcakes with Chocolate Stout Cream
    Cheese Frosting, 190–91
Chocolate Stout Whoopie Pies with Chocolate Cream
    Cheese Filling, 192–93
Cocoa and Stout Roasted Almonds, 122
Peanut Butter Stout Mousse-Topped Brownies, 196–97
Stout Chocolate Dipping Sauce, 186–87
Churros, beer, with chocolate stout sauce, 173–74
Cilantro Lime White Ale Vinaigrette, 160–61
Cinnamon rolls, miniature coffee stout, 198–99
Citrus
    Chipotle Lime Dipping Sauce, 171
    Honey-Orange Beer Glaze, 142–43
    IPA Lemon Bars, 202
    Orange Lime Gremolata, 153
Cocoa and Stout Roasted Almonds, 122
Coffee stout, in Miniature Coffee Stout Cinnamon Rolls,
    198–99
Condiments
    Garlic Beer Pickles, 25
    IPA Creole Mayo, 27
Cooking with beer, 13–16
    added shelf life and, 16
    heat intensification and, 16, 19, 21
    leavening and, 15
    meat tenderizing and, 15
    odds and ends, 16
    taste considerations, 14
Corn and cornmeal
    Garlic Beer–Butter Popcorn, 123
    Goat Cheese and Bacon Tarts with Pale Ale Polenta Crust, 130
    Jalapeño Cheddar Beer Hush Puppies, 176
    Salted Beer Caramel Corn, 124
Crab. See Seafood
Craft beer. See also Cooking with beer; specific beer types
    adding texture, 19
    celebrations of, 18
    glossary of terms, 205–12
    intensifying heat of dishes, 16, 19, 21
    intensity considerations, 19
    pairing with food, 19–20
    party themes, 20–21

popularity of, 18
recipes with. See specific beer types; specific main
    ingredients or types of foods
taste in recipes, 14
Cream, beer whipped, 200–201
Crispy Shallots and Parmesan Beer Cheese Dip, 83
Crostini, 60–76
    Beer-Braised Carnitas Crostini, 61–62
    Belgian Ale–Marinated Grilled Steak Crostini with IPA
        Chimichurri, 63–64
    Duck Confit Crostini with Porter Onion Jam and
        Pomegranates, 65–67
    Goat Cheese Crostini with Beer-Pickled Peaches, 68
    Parmesan Crab Beer Cheese Crostini, 71
    Peach Salsa and Beer-Battered Avocado Crostini, 72
    Porter Harissa Crostini, 69–70
    Smoked Salmon and Pale Ale Chive Cream Cheese
        Crostini, 73–74
    Spinach Artichoke Beer Cheese Crostini, 75
    Stout-Soaked Mushroom and Herbed Goat Cheese
        Crostini, 76
Cucumbers
    Garlic Beer Pickles, 25
    Seven-Layer Jalapeño IPA Hummus Dip, 88
    Yogurt Topping, 35
Curried Belgian Ale Mixed Nuts, 121

Dates, maple porter–glazed bacon-wrapped, 50–51
Deep-fried bites, 168–81
    Beer-Battered Avocado Fries, 169
    Beer-Battered Mini Corn Dogs, 170
    Beer-Battered Shrimp with Chipotle Lime Dipping Sauce, 171
    Beer-Battered Stout Pork Meatballs, 172
    Beer Churros with Chocolate Stout Sauce, 173–74
    Fried IPA Cheddar Mashed Potato Balls, 175
    Jalapeño Cheddar Beer Hush Puppies, 176
    Jalapeño Popper Beer Cheese Wontons, 177
    Raspberry Porter Jelly–Filled Beer Doughnuts, 178–79
    Tempura Beer-Battered Asparagus, 180–81
Desserts, 184–202
    Barrel-Aged Stout Marshmallows with Stout Chocolate
        Dipping Sauce, 186–87
    Beer Churros with Chocolate Stout Sauce, 173–74
    Belgian Ale Blackberry Sour Cream Ice Cream, 185
    Blueberry Beer Mini Pies, 188–89
    Chocolate Stout Cupcakes with Chocolate Stout Cream
        Cheese Frosting, 190–91

Desserts —*continued*
    Chocolate Stout Whoopie Pies with Chocolate Cream
        Cheese Filling, 192–93
    Grilled Apricots with Saison Mascarpone and Stout
        Balsamic Glaze, 194–95
    IPA Lemon Bars, 202
    Miniature Coffee Stout Cinnamon Rolls, 198–99
    Miniature Hefeweizen Pound Cakes with Beer Whipped
        Cream, 200–201
    Peanut Butter Stout Mousse-Topped Brownies, 196–97
    Raspberry Porter Jelly–Filled Beer Doughnuts, 178–79
Dips, **78**–91
    Beer and Bacon Dip, 79
    Buffalo Chicken Beer Cheese Dip, 80
    Chipotle Porter Hummus, 81–82
    Crispy Shallots and Parmesan Beer Cheese Dip, 83
    Pale Ale and Kale Tzatziki, 84–85
    Parsley White Bean Beer Cheese Dip, 86
    Porter Black Bean Dip, 87
    Roasted Garlic and Smoked Porter Baba Ghanoush, 90–91
    Seven-Layer Jalapeño IPA Hummus Dip, 88
    Triple-Chili Beer Cheese Dip, 89
Drunk Shrimp Diablo, 151
Duck Confit Crostini with Porter Onion Jam and
    Pomegranates, 65–67

Eggplant, in Roasted Garlic and Smoked Porter Baba
    Ghanoush, 90–91
Empanadas, chicken beer cheese pretzel, 102–4
Endive, in IPA Smoked Salmon Lettuce Wraps, 105

Figs, in Belgian Ale Ricotta Tarts with Roasted Figs and Honey
    Beer Caramel Sauce, 134–37
Fish. *See* Seafood
Flatbreads, grilled brie and prosciutto with honey-orange
    beer glaze, 142–43
Flavors of beer
    food taste and, 14, 19–20
    pairing with food, 19–20
Food, pairing beer with, 19–20. *See also specific recipes*
French dip sliders, stout, 39
Fried IPA Cheddar Mashed Potato Balls, 175
Fried Wonton Buns, 29–30
Fries, beer-battered avocado, 169

Garlic
    Garlic Beer-Butter Popcorn, 123

Garlic Beer Pickles, 25
Garlic Chili Beer Butter Shrimp, 158
Roasted Garlic and Smoked Porter Baba Ghanoush, 90–91
Roasted Garlic Beer Butter Shrimp Skewers, 52
Glossary of beer terms, 205–12
Goat Cheese and Bacon Tarts with Pale Ale Polenta Crust, 130
Goat Cheese Crostini with Beer-Pickled Peaches, 68
Gremolata, orange lime, 153
Grilled Barbecue Chicken and Peach Mini Pizzas, 140–41
Grilled Beer-Marinated Prosciutto-Wrapped Beef Tenderloin
    Skewers, 44
Grilled Prawns with Cilantro Lime White Ale Vinaigrette,
    160–61
Grilled Rosemary Porter Fillet Tip Skewers, 45–46
Growler potluck, 20
Guacamole
    Horseradish Guacamole, 37
    IPA Guacamole, 138–39

Handfuls, **112**–24
    Beer and Sriracha-Candied Nuts, 113–14
    Beer-Battered Gorgonzola-Stuffed Olives, 115
    Beer-Candied Pecans, 116
    Beer Sausage Stuffed–Crispy Fried Olives, 117
    Chili Lime Beer Roasted Peanuts, 118
    Chocolate and Stout-Coated Almonds, 119
    Cocoa and Stout Roasted Almonds, 122
    Curried Belgian Ale Mixed Nuts, 121
    Garlic Beer-Butter Popcorn, 123
    Salted Beer Caramel Corn, 124
Hand pies, wraps, and rolls, **94**–110
    Beer-Brined Chicken and Strawberry Salsa Lettuce Wraps, 95
    Beer-Caramelized Mushroom and Spinach Hand Pies, 98
    Beer Pesto and Beer Ricotta Mini Calzones, 96–97
    Blackberry Stout Wontons, 99
    Brown Ale Pork and Apple-Filled Buns, 100–101
    Chicken Beer Cheese Pretzel Empanadas, 102–4
    IPA Smoked Salmon Lettuce Wraps, 105
    Mushroom Stout Pork Hand Pies, 106–7
    Smoked Stout, Caramelized Onion, and Potato Pierogies, 108
    Tomato Beer Jam–Filled Biscuits, 109–10
Harissa crostini, porter, 69–70
Hawaiian IPA Pulled-Pork Sliders, 34
Heat, alcohol intensifying, 16
Heat, party theme around, 21
Hefeweizen, in Crab Salad Sliders on Pepper Beer Biscuits,
    32–33

Hoisin Stout–Braised Pork Rib Tarts, 144–45
Honey Beer Caramel Sauce, 134–35
Honey-Orange Beer Glaze, 142–43
Honey Stout Chicken Skewers, 47
Horseradish Guacamole, 37
Hot dogs, in Beer-Battered Mini Corn Dogs, 170
Hummus
    Chipotle Porter Hummus, 81–82
    IPA Hummus Dip, 88
Hush puppies, jalapeño cheddar beer, 176

Ice cream, Belgian ale blackberry sour cream, 185
Imperial stout, in Salted Beer Caramel Corn, 124
International Stout Day, 18
IPA
    Beer and Bacon Dip, 79
    Beer and Sriracha–Candied Nuts, 113–14
    Beer-Battered Mini Corn Dogs, 170
    Beer-Battered Shrimp Po' Boy Sliders with IPA Creole
        Mayo, 27–28
    Beer-Braised Carnitas Crostini, 61–62
    Beer-Candied Pecans, 116
    Belgian Ale–Marinated Grilled Steak Crostini with IPA
        Chimichurri, 63–64
    Blackened Beer-Brined Chicken Masa Tarts with IPA
        Guacamole, 138–39
    Buffalo Chicken Beer Cheese Dip, 80
    Chili Lime Beer Roasted Peanuts, 118
    Crab Salad, 32–33
    Drunk Shrimp Diablo, 151
    Fried IPA Cheddar Mashed Potato Balls, 175
    Garlic Chili Beer Butter Shrimp, 158
    Hawaiian IPA Pulled-Pork Sliders, 34
    IPA Chimichurri, 63
    IPA Guacamole, 138–39
    IPA Lemon Bars, 202
    IPA Smoked Salmon Lettuce Wraps, 105
    IPA-Soaked Watermelon Skewers with Cotija and Mint,
        48–49
    Jalapeño Popper Beer Cheese Wontons, 177
    Mango Shrimp IPA Ceviche in Baked Wonton Cups, 159
    Parmesan Crab Beer Cheese Crostini, 71
    Parsley White Bean Beer Cheese Dip, 86
    Peach Salsa and Beer-Battered Avocado Crostini, 72
    Seven-Layer Jalapeño IPA Hummus Dip, 88
    Spinach Artichoke Beer Cheese Crostini, 75
    Triple-Chili Beer Cheese Dip, 89

IPA Creole Mayo, 27
IPA Day, 18

Jalapeño Cheddar Beer Hush Puppies, 176
Jalapeño Popper Beer Cheese Wontons, 177
Jam-filled biscuits, tomato beer, 109–10

Kale, in Pale Ale and Kale Tzatziki, 84–85

Lamb, in Beer-Braised Lamb Shank Tarts with Belgian Cherry
    Sauce, 127–29
Leavening, 15
Lemon bars, IPA, 202
Lettuce wraps
    Beer-Brined Chicken and Strawberry Salsa Lettuce Wraps, 95
    IPA Smoked Salmon Lettuce Wraps, 105
Lobster. See Seafood

Mango Shrimp IPA Ceviche in Baked Wonton Cups, 159
Maple Porter–Glazed Bacon-Wrapped Dates, 50–51
Marshmallows, barrel-aged stout, with stout chocolate
    dipping sauce, 186–87
Mashed potato balls, fried IPA cheddar, 175
Mayo, IPA Creole, 27
Measurement conversion chart, 203
Meat, tenderizing, 15
Meatballs
    Beer-Battered Stout Pork Meatballs, 172
    Salmon Meatballs with Asian Porter Sauce, 164–65
Mediterranean Beer-Braised Pork Sliders, 35
Melon
    Beer-Soaked Cantaloupe and Mozzarella Skewers, 43
    IPA-Soaked Watermelon Skewers with Cotija and Mint,
        48–49
Metric conversion chart, 203
Miniature Coffee Stout Cinnamon Rolls, 198–99
Miniature Hefeweizen Pound Cakes with Beer Whipped
    Cream, 200–201
Mint, in IPA-Soaked Watermelon Skewers with Cotija and
    Mint, 48–49
Miso Ale–Glazed Shrimp, 166
Miso Stout Salmon Spring Rolls, 162–63
Mousse-topped brownies, peanut butter stout, 196–97
Mushrooms
    Beer-Caramelized Mushroom and Spinach Hand Pies, 98
    Beer–Caramelized Mushroom Gorgonzola Tart, 146
    Mushroom Stout Pork Hand Pies, 106–7

Mushrooms—*continued*
  Stout-Soaked Mushroom and Herbed Goat Cheese Crostini, 76
National Beer Day, 18
Nuts and seeds
  Beer and Sriracha–Candied Nuts, 113–14
  Beer-Candied Pecans, 116
  Beer Peanut Sauce, 56
  Beer Pesto and Beer Ricotta Mini Calzones, 96–97
  Chili Lime Beer Roasted Peanuts, 118
  Chocolate and Stout–Coated Almonds, 119
  Cocoa and Stout Roasted Almonds, 122
  Curried Belgian Ale Mixed Nuts, 121
  Peanut Butter Stout Mousse–Topped Brownies, 196–97

Olives
  Beer-Battered Gorgonzola-Stuffed Olives, 115
  Beer Sausage Stuffed–Crispy Fried Olives, 117
Onions
  Belgian Ale–Caramelized Apple and Onion Tarts, 131–33
  Onion Jam, 65
  Smoked Stout, Caramelized Onion, and Potato Pierogies, 108

Pairing beer and food, 19–20. *See also specific recipes*
Pale ale
  Beer Pesto and Beer Ricotta Mini Calzones, 96–97
  Beer-Poached Lobster Sliders, 31
  Beer Sausage Stuffed–Crispy Fried Olives, 117
  Blackened Beer-Brined Chicken Masa Tarts with IPA
    Guacamole, 138–39
  Garlic Beer–Butter Popcorn, 123
  Goat Cheese and Bacon Tarts with Pale Ale Polenta Crust, 130
  Goat Cheese Crostini with Beer-Pickled Peaches, 68
  Jalapeño Cheddar Beer Hush Puppies, 176
  Miso Ale–Glazed Shrimp, 166
  Pale Ale and Kale Tzatziki, 84–85
  Smoked Salmon and Pale Ale Chive Cream Cheese
    Crostini, 73–74
  Yogurt and Beer–Marinated Chicken Skewers, 58
Parmesan Crab Beer Cheese Crostini, 71
Parsley White Bean Beer Cheese Dip, 86
Party themes, 20–21
  growler potluck, 20
  some like it hot, 21
  sugar shindig, 20–21
Peaches
  Beer-Pickled Peaches, 68
  Grilled Barbecue Chicken and Peach Mini Pizzas, 140–41

Peach Salsa and Beer-Battered Avocado Crostini, 72
Peanuts. *See* Nuts and seeds
Pepper(s)
  about: alcohol intensifying heat of, 16, 19, 21
  Chipotle Lime Dipping Sauce, 171
  Chipotle Porter Hummus, 81–82
  Jalapeño Cheddar Beer Hush Puppies, 176
  Jalapeño Popper Beer Cheese Wontons, 177
  Pepper Beer Biscuits, 32–33
  Porter Harissa Crostini, 69–70
  Triple-Chili Beer Cheese Dip, 89
Pickles
  Beer-Pickled Peaches, 68
  Garlic Beer Pickles, 25
Pierogies, smoked stout, caramelized onion and potato, 108
Pies. *See* Desserts; Hand pies, wraps, and rolls; Tartlets and
  mini pies
Pilsner, in Beer-Steamed Clams with Linguiça, 156–57
Pizzas, peach mini, and grilled barbecue chicken, 140–41
Plums, in Porter-Soaked Plum, Bacon, and Arugula Tarts,
  147–48
Pomegranates, duck confit crostini with porter onion jam
  and, 65–67
Popcorn
  Garlic Beer–Butter Popcorn, 123
  Salted Beer Caramel Corn, 124
Popularity, of craft beer, 18
Pork
  about: beer/alcohol tenderizing, 15
  Beer and Bacon Dip, 79
  Beer-Battered Mini Corn Dogs, 170
  Beer-Battered Stout Pork Meatballs, 172
  Beer-Braised Asian Pork Sliders with Fried Wonton Buns,
    29–30
  Beer-Braised Carnitas Crostini, 61–62
  Beer Sausage Stuffed–Crispy Fried Olives, 117
  Beer-Steamed Clams with Linguiça, 156–57
  Brown Ale Pork and Apple–Filled Buns, 100–101
  Goat Cheese and Bacon Tarts with Pale Ale Polenta Crust, 130
  Grilled Beer-Marinated Prosciutto-Wrapped Beef
    Tenderloin Skewers, 44
  Grilled Brie and Prosciutto Flatbreads with Honey-Orange
    Beer Glaze, 142–43
  Hawaiian IPA Pulled-Pork Sliders, 34
  Hoisin Stout–Braised Pork Rib Tarts, 144–45
  Maple Porter–Glazed Bacon-Wrapped Dates, 50–51
  Mediterranean Beer-Braised Pork Sliders, 35

Mushroom Stout Pork Hand Pies, 106–7
Pork Stout Meatball Banh Mi Sliders, 36
Porter Pulled-Pork Sliders with Horseradish Guacamole, 37
Porter-Soaked Plum, Bacon, and Arugula Tarts, 147–48
Porter
    Chipotle Porter Hummus, 81–82
    Duck Confit Crostini with Porter Onion Jam and
        Pomegranates, 65–67
    Grilled Beer-Marinated Prosciutto-Wrapped Beef
        Tenderloin Skewers, 44
    Grilled Rosemary Porter Fillet Tip Skewers, 45–46
    Maple Porter-Glazed Bacon-Wrapped Dates, 50–51
    Mediterranean Beer-Braised Pork Sliders, 35
    Porter Black Bean Dip, 87
    Porter Harissa Crostini, 69–70
    Porter Pulled-Pork Sliders with Horseradish Guacamole, 37
    Porter-Soaked Plum, Bacon, and Arugula Tarts, 147–48
    Raspberry Porter Jelly–Filled Beer Doughnuts, 178–79
    Roasted Garlic and Smoked Porter Baba Ghanoush, 90–91
    Salmon Meatballs with Asian Porter Sauce, 164–65
    Smoky Porter Molasses Chicken Skewers, 53–55
Potatoes
    Fried IPA Cheddar Mashed Potato Balls, 175
    Smoked Stout, Caramelized Onion, and Potato Pierogies, 108
Potluck, growler, 20
Poultry
    about: beer/alcohol tenderizing, 15
    Barbecue Chicken Sliders with Garlic Beer Pickles, 25–26
    Beer-Brined Chicken and Strawberry Salsa Lettuce Wraps, 95
    Blackened Beer-Brined Chicken Masa Tarts with IPA
        Guacamole, 138–39
    Buffalo Chicken Beer Cheese Dip, 80
    Chicken Beer Cheese Pretzel Empanadas, 102–4
    Duck Confit Crostini with Porter Onion Jam and
        Pomegranates, 65–67
    Grilled Barbecue Chicken and Peach Mini Pizzas, 140–41
    Honey Stout Chicken Skewers, 47
    Smoky Porter Molasses Chicken Skewers, 53–55
    Yogurt and Beer-Marinated Chicken Skewers, 58
Pretzel empanadas, chicken beer cheese, 102–4
Prosciutto
    Grilled Beer-Marinated Prosciutto-Wrapped Beef
        Tenderloin Skewers, 44
    Grilled Brie and Prosciutto Flatbreads with Honey-Orange
        Beer Glaze, 142–43

Raspberry Porter Jelly–Filled Beer Doughnuts, 178–79

Red ale, in Beer–Caramelized Mushroom Gorgonzola Tart, 146
Roasted Garlic and Smoked Porter Baba Ghanoush, 90–91
Roasted Garlic Beer Butter Shrimp Skewers, 52
Rolls. See Hand pies, wraps, and rolls

Saison
    Beer and Butter-Poached Scallops with Orange Lime
        Gremolata, 152–53
    Grilled Apricots with Saison Mascarpone and Stout
        Balsamic Glaze, 194–95
    Roasted Garlic Beer Butter Shrimp Skewers, 52
Salmon. See Seafood
Salted Beer Caramel Corn, 124
Sauces and frostings
    Asian Porter Sauce, 164
    Beer Peanut Sauce, 56
    Beer Pesto, 96–97
    Beer Whipped Cream, 200–201
    Belgian Cherry Sauce, 127–29
    Chipotle Lime Dipping Sauce, 171
    Chocolate Stout Cream Cheese Frosting, 190–91
    Chocolate Stout Sauce, 173
    Cilantro Lime White Ale Vinaigrette, 160–61
    Cinnamon Roll Frosting, 198–99
    Honey Beer Caramel Sauce, 134–35
    Honey-Orange Beer Glaze, 142–43
    Horseradish Guacamole, 37
    IPA Chimichurri, 63
    Onion Jam, 65
    Peach Salsa, 72
    Stout Balsamic Glaze, 195
    Stout Chocolate Dipping Sauce, 186–87
    Strawberry Salsa, 95
    Yogurt Topping, 35
Sausage
    Beer Sausage Stuffed–Crispy Fried Olives, 117
    Beer-Steamed Clams with Linguiça, 156–57
Seafood, 150–66
    about: beer/alcohol tenderizing, 15
    Beer and Butter-Poached Scallops with Orange Lime
        Gremolata, 152–53
    Beer-Battered Crab Beignets, 154–55
    Beer-Battered Shrimp Po' Boy Sliders with IPA Creole
        Mayo, 27–28
    Beer-Battered Shrimp with Chipotle Lime Dipping Sauce, 171
    Beer-Poached Lobster Sliders, 31
    Beer-Steamed Clams with Linguiça, 156–57

Seafood—*continued*

    Crab Salad Sliders on Pepper Beer Biscuits, 32–33

    Drunk Shrimp Diablo, 151

    Garlic Chili Beer Butter Shrimp, 158

    Grilled Prawns with Cilantro Lime White Ale Vinaigrette, 160–61

    IPA Smoked Salmon Lettuce Wraps, 105

    Mango Shrimp IPA Ceviche in Baked Wonton Cups, 159

    Miso Ale–Glazed Shrimp, 166

    Miso Stout Salmon Spring Rolls, 162–63

    Parmesan Crab Beer Cheese Crostini, 71

    Roasted Garlic Beer Butter Shrimp Skewers, 52

    Salmon Meatballs with Asian Porter Sauce, 164–65

    Smoked Salmon and Pale Ale Chive Cream Cheese Crostini, 73–74

Seasonal party, 20

Seven-Layer Jalapeño IPA Hummus Dip, 88

Shallots, crispy, and parmesan beer cheese dip, 83

Shrimp. *See* Seafood

Skewers, **42**–58

    Beer-Soaked Cantaloupe and Mozzarella Skewers, 43

    Grilled Beer-Marinated Prosciutto-Wrapped Beef Tenderloin Skewers, 44

    Grilled Rosemary Porter Fillet Tip Skewers, 45–46

    Honey Stout Chicken Skewers, 47

    IPA-Soaked Watermelon Skewers with Cotija and Mint, 48–49

    Maple Porter–Glazed Bacon-Wrapped Dates, 50–51

    Roasted Garlic Beer Butter Shrimp Skewers, 52

    Smoky Porter Molasses Chicken Skewers, 53–55

    Stout-Marinated Beef Satay with Beer Peanut Sauce, 56–57

    Yogurt and Beer–Marinated Chicken Skewers, 58

Sliders, **24**–39

    Barbecue Chicken Sliders with Garlic Beer Pickles, 25–26

    Beer-Battered Shrimp Po' Boy Sliders with IPA Creole Mayo, 27–28

    Beer-Braised Asian Pork Sliders with Fried Wonton Buns, 29–30

    Beer-Poached Lobster Sliders, 31

    Crab Salad Sliders on Pepper Beer Biscuits, 32–33

    Hawaiian IPA Pulled-Pork Sliders, 34

    Mediterranean Beer-Braised Pork Sliders, 35

    Pork Stout Meatball Banh Mi Sliders, 36

    Porter Pulled-Pork Sliders with Horseradish Guacamole, 37

    Stout French Dip Sliders, 39

Smoked Salmon and Pale Ale Chive Cream Cheese Crostini, 73–74

Smoky Porter Molasses Chicken Skewers, 53–55

Spinach

    Beer-Caramelized Mushroom and Spinach Hand Pies, 98

    Spinach Artichoke Beer Cheese Crostini, 75

Spring rolls, miso stout, 162–63

Stout

    Barbecue Chicken Sliders with Garlic Beer Pickles, 25–26

    Barrel-Aged Stout Marshmallows with Stout Chocolate Dipping Sauce, 186–87

    Beer-Battered Stout Pork Meatballs, 172

    Blackberry Stout Wontons, 99

    Chocolate and Stout–Coated Almonds, 119

    Chocolate Stout Cupcakes with Chocolate Stout Cream Cheese Frosting, 190–91

    Chocolate Stout Whoopie Pies with Chocolate Cream Cheese Filling, 192–93

    Cocoa and Stout Roasted Almonds, 122

    Hoisin Stout–Braised Pork Rib Tarts, 144–45

    Honey Stout Chicken Skewers, 47

    Miso Stout Salmon Spring Rolls, 162–63

    Mushroom Stout Pork Hand Pies, 106–7

    Peanut Butter Stout Mousse–Topped Brownies, 196–97

    Pork Stout Meatball Banh Mi Sliders, 36

    Salted Beer Caramel Corn, 124

    Smoked Stout, Caramelized Onion, and Potato Pierogies, 108

    Stout Balsamic Glaze, 195

    Stout Chocolate Dipping Sauce, 186–87

    Stout French Dip Sliders, 39

    Stout-Marinated Beef Satay with Beer Peanut Sauce, 56–57

    Stout-Soaked Mushroom and Herbed Goat Cheese Crostini, 76

Stout (coffee), in Miniature Coffee Stout Cinnamon Rolls, 198–99

Strawberry Salsa, 95

Sugar shindig, 20–21

Summer ale

    Beer-Soaked Cantaloupe and Mozzarella Skewers, 43

    Grilled Brie and Prosciutto Flatbreads with Honey-Orange Beer Glaze, 142–43

    Honey-Orange Beer Glaze, 142–43

Tartlets and mini pies, **126**–48

    Beer-Braised Lamb Shank Tarts with Belgian Cherry Sauce, 127–29

    Beer-Caramelized Mushroom Gorgonzola Tart, 146

    Belgian Ale–Caramelized Apple and Onion Tarts, 131–33

Belgian Ale Ricotta Tarts with Roasted Figs and Honey Beer Caramel Sauce, 134–37

Blackened Beer-Brined Chicken Masa Tarts with IPA Guacamole, 138–39

Goat Cheese and Bacon Tarts with Pale Ale Polenta Crust, 130

Grilled Barbecue Chicken and Peach Mini Pizzas, 140–41

Grilled Brie and Prosciutto Flatbreads with Honey-Orange Beer Glaze, 142–43

Hoisin Stout–Braised Pork Rib Tarts, 144–45

Porter-Soaked Plum, Bacon, and Arugula Tarts, 147–48

Taste, of beer in recipes, 14, 19

Tempura Beer-Battered Asparagus, 180–81

Tenderizing meat, 15

Terms, glossary of, 205–12

Texture, from craft beer, 19

Tomato Beer Jam–Filled Biscuits, 109–10

Triple-Chili Beer Cheese Dip, 89

Tzatziki, pale ale and kale, 84–85

Watermelon, IPA-soaked skewers with cotija and mint, 48–49

Wheat beer

Beer-Battered Avocado Fries, 169

Beer-Battered Crab Beignets, 154–55

Beer-Battered Gorgonzola-Stuffed Olives, 115

Beer-Braised Asian Pork Sliders with Fried Wonton Buns, 29–30

Beer Churros with Chocolate Stout Sauce, 173–74

Chicken Beer Cheese Pretzel Empanadas, 102–4

Grilled Barbecue Chicken and Peach Mini Pizzas, 140–41

Miniature Hefeweizen Pound Cakes with Beer Whipped Cream, 200–201

Tempura Beer-Battered Asparagus, 180–81

Tomato Beer Jam–Filled Biscuits, 109–10

Whipped cream, beer, 200–201

White ale, in Grilled Prawns with Cilantro Lime White Ale Vinaigrette, 160–61

Wonton buns, fried, 29–30

Wontons

Blackberry Stout Wontons, 99

Jalapeño Popper Beer Cheese Wontons, 177

Mango Shrimp IPA Ceviche in Baked Wonton Cups, 159

Wraps. *See* Hand pies, wraps, and rolls

Yogurt

Yogurt and Beer–Marinated Chicken Skewers, 58

Yogurt Topping, 35